The Art of Horsemanship

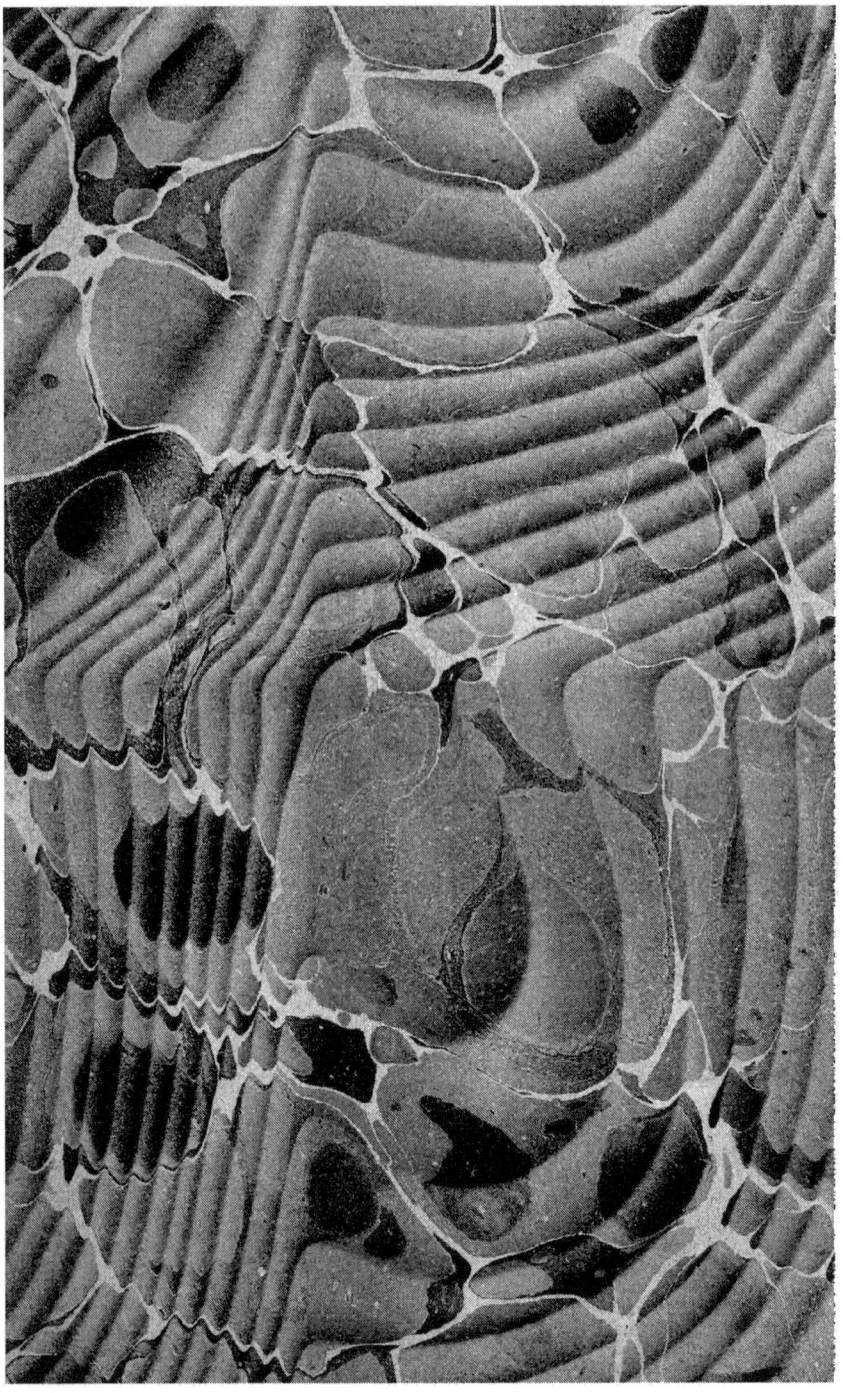

Willis Munro.
June 1899.

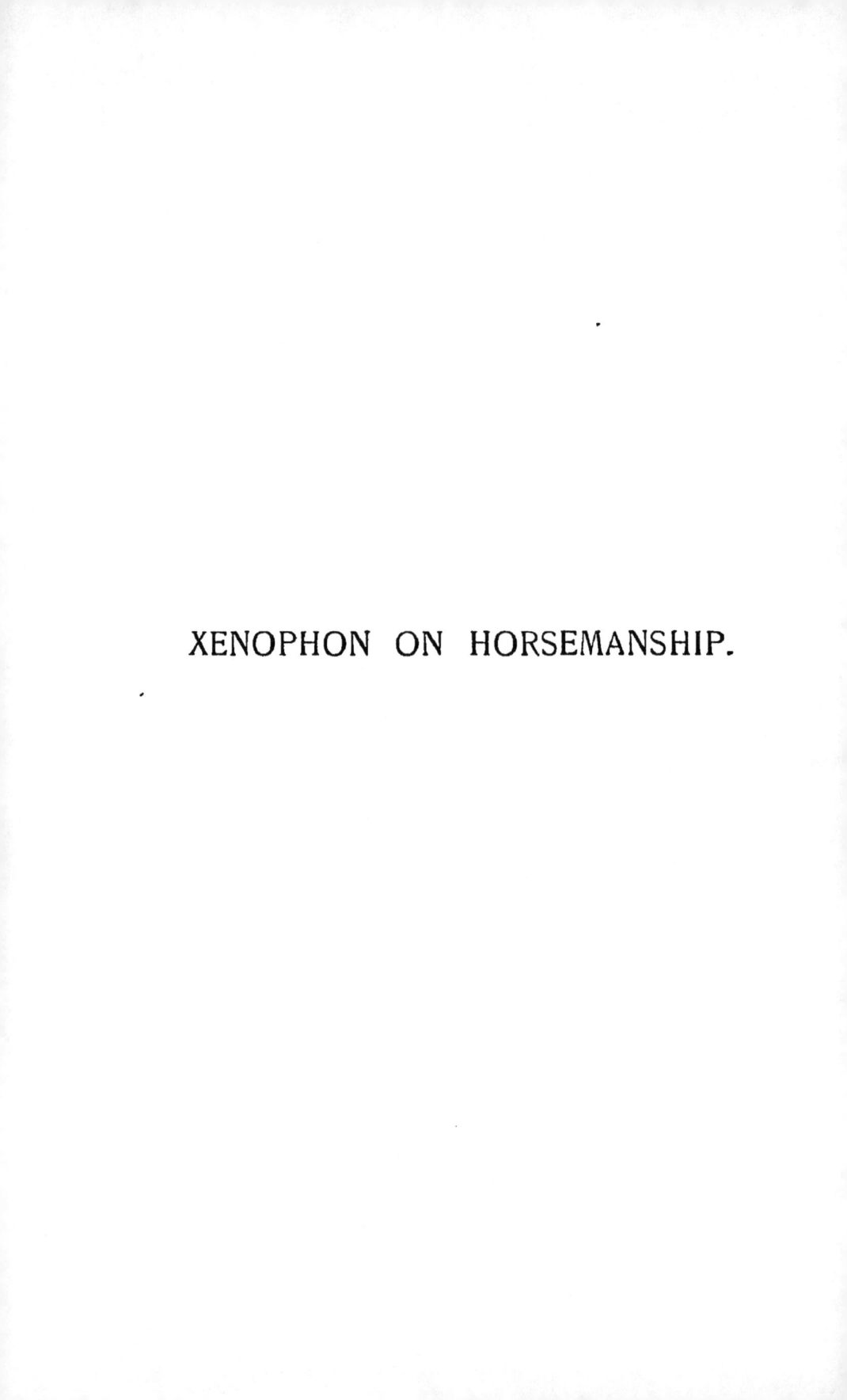

XENOPHON ON HORSEMANSHIP.

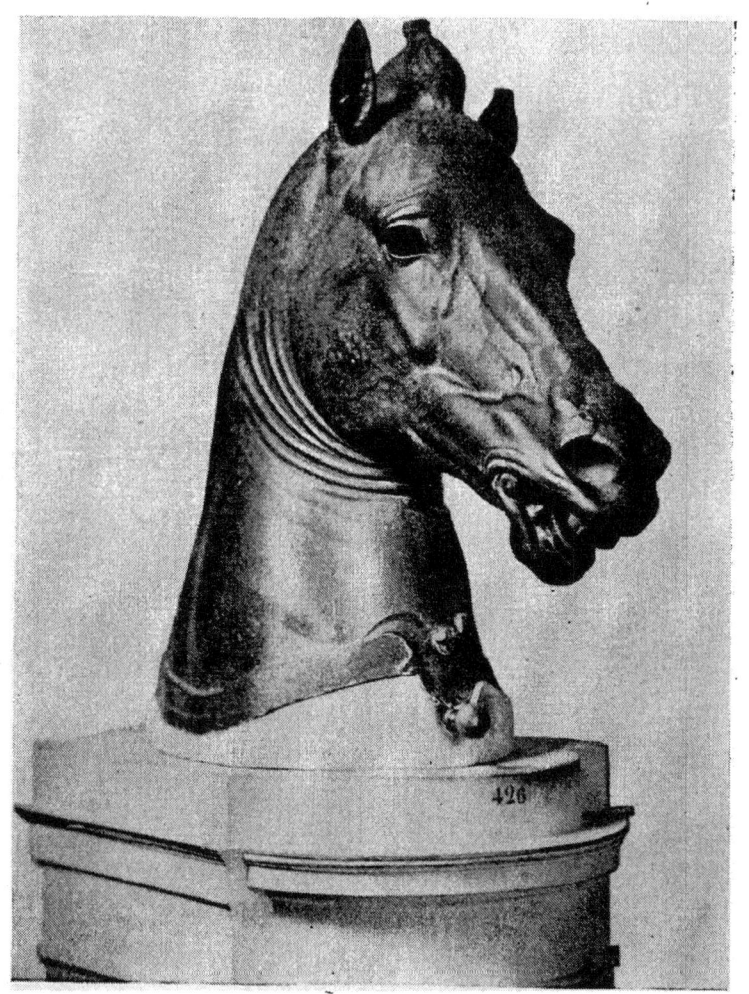

THE ART

OF

HORSEMANSHIP.

BY

XENOPHON.

TRANSLATED, WITH CHAPTERS ON THE GREEK RIDING-HORSE
AND WITH NOTES,

BY

MORRIS H. MORGAN, Ph.D.

Assistant Professor in Harvard University.

Proficies nihil hoc, caedas licet usque, flagello.

BOSTON:
LITTLE, BROWN, AND COMPANY.
1893.

THE ART

OF

HORSEMANSHIP.

BY

XENOPHON.

TRANSLATED, WITH CHAPTERS ON THE GREEK RIDING-HORSE
AND WITH NOTES,

BY

MORRIS H. MORGAN, Ph.D.

Assistant Professor in Harvard University

Proficies nihil hoc, caedas licet usque, flagello.

BOSTON:
LITTLE, BROWN, AND COMPANY.
1893.

Copyright, 1893,
By Morris H. Morgan.

𝔘𝔫𝔦𝔳𝔢𝔯𝔰𝔦𝔱𝔶 𝔓𝔯𝔢𝔰𝔰:
John Wilson and Son, Cambridge, U.S.A.

PREFACE.

AMONG technical treatises, that of Xenophon on Horsemanship is almost unique in one particular. Even after more than twenty-three centuries it is still, in the main, a sound and excellent guide for so much of the field as it covers. This fact, together with the simple and delightful manner in which the subject is treated, has led me to think that some who are not able or do not care to approach the book in the original Greek, might like to read a translation of the earliest known work on the horse and how to ride him. To be sure, there have already been versions in English; but these seem to me, and have seemed to others, unsatisfactory.

My translation is made from the Greek text of Dindorf's Oxford edition. Two well-known special editions of the treatise I have found very useful. These are by Courier, with notes and a translation into French, first published in Paris in 1813, and by Jacobs, with notes and a German version, Gotha, 1825. Hermann's essay, "De verbis quibus Graeci incessum equorum indicant," is indispensable for the study of certain parts of the treatise. I have also consulted the German translation of Ginzrot, with brief notes, in the second volume of his large work called "Die Wagen und Fuhrwerke der Griechen und Römer," Munich, 1817. Ginzrot's book must be used with caution; the illustrations are often fanciful, and the statements need verification; but his translation of Xenophon is sometimes helpful. In English I have seen three translations, — Berenger's (in his "History and Art of Horsemanship," London, 1771, a somewhat rare book, for the loan of which I am obliged to the Librarian of the Boston Athenaeum); an anonymous translation reprinted with the minor works of Xenophon in Philadelphia in 1845; and Watson's, in Bohn's Classical Library. The first is by far the best, but I have not found either of the three of much

PREFACE. vii

assistance. There has been no edition of the Greek text with English notes.

The illustrations in this book are all selected from the antique, and are reproduced from the best sources at my command. These sources, together with a brief description of each picture, are given on page 158 ff. I might have illustrated almost every subject in the treatise by means of the Parthenon frieze; but I choose rather to omit all but a few of these well-known works, and to present others which are less generally known to the readers for whom my book is primarily intended. For it will be easy to see that I have not written for philologians. The brief essay on the Greek Riding-horse makes no pretence to completeness, and little to originality. In it, and in the notes which follow, my chief intention has been to offer only what I thought would be necessary explanation or interesting information to those who do not profess to be classical scholars. Yet perhaps even such scholars may find here and there, especially in the notes, a few points which may be new, and, I hope, not unacceptable to them. And I sincerely wish that this little book might lead some one to a more thorough study of the subjects of riding and driving in antiquity. They offer a fertile and interesting field for special investigation.

Besides the German works already mentioned, and the ordinary classical handbooks, the best books in which to find information about the Greek horse and horsemanship are Schlieben's "Die Pferde des Altertums," 1867, Martin's "Les Cavaliers Athéniens," 1886, and Daremberg and Saglio's "Dictionnaire des Antiquités," under the words *equites*, *equus*, etc. I have not seen Lehndorf's "Hippodromos," 1876, nor Piétrement's "Les chevaux dans les temps historiques et préhistoriques," 1883. One of the most charming of the works of Cherbuliez is his "Cheval de Phidias," 1864, in which the subject is considered from purely artistic and aesthetic points of view. Of course there is much information scattered through periodical literature; but, in spite of all, the book of the ancient horse is yet to be written.

M. H. M.

May, 1893.

CONTENTS.

	PAGE
XENOPHON ON HORSEMANSHIP	13
THE GREEK RIDING-HORSE	69
POINTS OF THE HORSE	107
NOTES	119
ON THE ILLUSTRATIONS	159
INDEX	185

XENOPHON ON HORSEMANSHIP.

CHAPTER I.

IT has been my fortune to spend a great deal of time in riding, and so I think myself versed in the horseman's art. This makes me willing to set forth to the younger of my friends what I believe would be the best way for them to deal with horses. It is true that a book on horsemanship has already been written by Simon:[1] I mean the man who dedicated the bronze horse at the Eleusinion[2] in Athens with his own exploits

[1] The numerals refer to the Notes, p. 119 ff.

in relief on the pedestal. Still, I shall not strike out of my work all the points in which I chance to agree with him, but shall take much greater pleasure in passing them on to my friends, believing that I speak with the more authority because a famous horseman, such as he, has thought as I do. And then, again, I shall try to make clear whatever he has omitted.

To begin with, I shall describe how a man, in buying a horse, would be least likely to be cheated. In the case of an unbroken colt, of course his frame is what you must test; as for spirit, no very sure signs of that are offered by an animal that has never yet been mounted. And in his frame, the first things which I say you ought to look at are his feet.[3] Just as a house would be good for nothing if it were very handsome above but lacked the proper foundations, so too a war-horse, even if all his other points were fine, would yet be good for nothing if he had bad feet; for he could not use a single one of his fine points.

The feet should first be tested by examining the horn; thick horn[4] is a much better

CHAPTER I.   15

mark of good feet than thin. Again, one should not fail to note whether the hoofs at toe and heel come up high or lie low. High ones keep what is called the frog[5] well off the ground, while horses with low hoofs walk with the hardest and softest part of the foot at once, like knock-kneed men. Simon says that their sound is a proof of good feet, and he is right; for a hollow hoof resounds like a cymbal as it strikes the ground.

As we have begun here, let us now proceed to the rest of the body. The bones above the hoofs and below the fetlocks should not be very straight up and down, like the goat's; for if they have no spring, they jar the rider, and such legs are apt to get inflamed. These bones should not come down very low, either, else the horse might get his fetlocks stripped of hair[6] and torn in riding over heavy ground or over stones. The shank bones ought to be stout, for they are the supporters of the body; but they should not be thickly coated with flesh or veins: if they are, in riding over hard ground the veins would fill with blood and become varicose, the legs would swell, and the flesh recede. With this slackening of the flesh, the back sinew[7] often gives way, and makes the horse lame. As for the knees, if they are supple in bending when the colt walks, you may infer that his limbs will be supple in riding; for as time goes on, all colts get more and more supple at the knees. Supple knees are highly esteemed; and justly, because they make the horse easier and less likely to stumble than stiff ones. Forearms[8] stout below the shoulders look stronger and comelier, as they do in man.

The broader the chest so much the handsomer and the stronger is it, and the more naturally adapted to carry the legs well apart and without interference. The neck should not be thrown out from the chest like a boar's, but, like a cock's, should rise straight up to the poll and be slim at the bend, while the head, though bony, should have but a small jaw.[9] The neck would then protect the rider, and the eye see what lies before the feet. A horse thus shaped could do the least harm, even if he were very high-spirited; for it is not by arching the neck and head, but by stretching them out, that horses try their powers of violence. You

should note also whether his jaws are fine or hard, whether they are alike or different.[10] Horses whose jaws are unlike are generally hard-mouthed. A prominent eye rather than a sunken one is a sure sign that the horse is wide awake; and such a one can see farther too. Wide nostrils[11] mean freer breathing than close ones, and at the same time they make the horse look fiercer; for whenever a horse is provoked at another or gets excited during exercise, he dilates his nostrils very widely.

A rather large poll[12] and ears somewhat small give the head more of the look which a horse should have. High withers make the rider's seat surer, and his grip on the shoulders stronger. A double back[13] is easier to sit upon, and better looking than a single one. A deep side, rather rounded at the belly, generally makes the horse at once easier to sit upon, stronger, and a better feeder. The broader and the shorter the loins, with so much the greater ease does the horse raise his forehand and bring up the hind-quarters to follow; then, too, the belly looks smallest, which, when it is large, is not only disfiguring, but makes the horse weaker and more unwieldy. The quarters should be broad and full in proportion to the sides and chest; and all these parts, if firm, would be lighter for running, and make your horse a great deal faster. If he has his buttocks well apart under the tail with the line between them broad, he will be sure to spread well behind; in so doing he will have a stronger and a prouder look, both when gathering himself in [14] and in riding, and all his points will be improved. You may take the case of men to prove this; whenever they wish to lift anything from the ground, they do it with their legs apart rather than close together. The horse should certainly not have large stones; but this point cannot be determined in the colt. As for the hocks below, or the shanks and the fetlocks and hoofs, I say about them here just what I did in the case of the forefeet.

I will set down, too, how you are least likely to miss the mark in the matter of size. That colt always turns out the largest whose shanks are longest at the time of foaling. For the shanks do not grow [15] very much in any quadrupeds as time goes on, but the rest of the frame grows so as to correspond to the shanks. It seems to me that, by testing a colt's shape in the manner described, people would get, as a general rule, an animal with sound feet, strong, good-conditioned, graceful, and large. Even though some alter as they grow, we should still apply these tests with confidence, since there are a great many more ugly colts that turn out handsome than handsome ones that turn out ugly.

CHAPTER II.

IT does not seem necessary for me to describe the method of breaking a colt, because those who are enlisted in the cavalry [16] in our states are persons of very considerable means, and take no small part in the government. It is also a great deal better than being a horse-breaker for a young man to see that his own condition and that of his horse is good, or if he knows this already, to keep up his practice in riding; while an old man had better attend to his family and friends, to public business and military matters, than be spending his time in horse-breaking.

CHAPTER II.

The man, then, that feels as I do about horse-breaking will, of course, put out his colt. He should not put him out, however, without having a written contract made, stating what the horse is to be taught before he is returned, just as he does when he puts his son out to learn a trade. This will serve as a reminder to the horse-breaker of what he must attend to, if he is to get his fee.

See to it that the colt be kind, used to the hand, and fond of men when he is put out to the horse-breaker. He is generally made so at home and by the groom, if the man knows how to manage so that solitude means to the colt hunger and thirst and teasing horseflies, while food, drink, and relief from pain come from man. For if this be done, colts must not only love men, but even long for them. Then, too, the horse should be stroked in the places which he most likes to have handled; that is, where the hair is thickest, and where he is least able to help himself if anything hurts him. The groom should also be directed to lead him through crowds, and to make him familiar with all sorts of sights and all sorts of noises. Whenever the colt is frightened at any of them, he should be taught, not by irritating but by soothing him, that there is nothing to fear. It seems to me that this is enough to tell the amateur to do in the matter of horse-breaking.

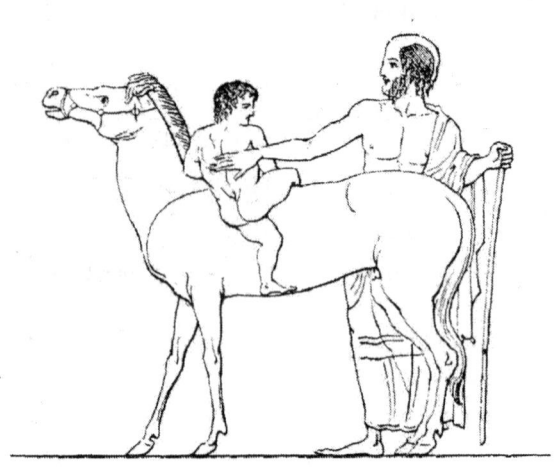

CHAPTER III.

I SHALL now set down some memoranda to be observed in buying a horse already broken to riding, if you are not to be cheated in the purchase. First, then, the question of age should not pass unnoticed; for if he no longer has the markers,[17] the prospect is not a glad one, and he is not to be disposed of so easily. His youth once made sure of, the way in which he lets you put the bit into his mouth, and the head-piece about his ears, should not escape you. This would be least likely to pass unnoticed if the bridle were put on and taken off in the sight of the purchaser. Next we ought to observe how he receives the rider upon his back; a good many horses hardly let come near them things whose very approach is a sign that there is work to be done. This, too, must be observed, — whether, when mounted, he is willing to leave other horses, or whether, when ridden near horses that are standing still, he runs away towards them. Some horses, also, from bad training take flight towards home from the riding-grounds. The exercise called the Volte [18] shows up a hard mouth, and even more the practice of changing the direction. Many horses do not try to run away unless the mouth is hard on the same side with the road for a bolt towards home.[19] Then you must know whether, when let out at full speed, he will come to the poise and be willing to turn round. It is not a bad thing to try whether he is just as ready to mind when roused by a blow as he was before. A disobedient servant is of course a useless thing, and so is a disobedient army; a disobedient horse is not only useless, but he often plays the part of a very traitor.

CHAPTER III.

As I assume that the horse to be bought is meant for war, trial should be made of all the qualities that war itself puts to the test. These are jumping ditches, going over walls, breasting banks, and leaping down from them; you must try him riding up hill and down dale and along the slope. All these tests prove whether his spirit is strong and his body sound. He should not be rejected, however, if he does not perform them all very finely; as many animals fail, not from inability but from want of practice in these feats. With instruction, habit, and practice they may do all finely, provided they are sound and not vicious. But you must beware of horses that are naturally shy. The over-timid let no harm come to the enemy from off their backs, and they often throw the rider and bring him into the greatest danger.

You must learn, too, whether the horse has any particular vice, shown towards other horses or towards men, and whether he is very skittish. These are all troublesome matters for his owner. You could much better discover objections to being bridled and mounted and other vices, by trying to do over again, after the horse has finished his work, just what you did before beginning your ride. Horses that are ready to submit to a task the second time, after having done it once, give proof enough of high spirit. To sum it all up, the least troublesome and the most serviceable to his rider in the wars would naturally be the horse that is sound-footed, gentle, sufficiently fleet, ready and able to undergo fatigue, and, first and foremost, obedient. On the other hand, horses that need much urging from laziness or much coaxing and attention from being too mettlesome, keep the rider's hands always engaged, and take away his courage in moments of danger.

CHAPTER IV.

WHEN one has bought a horse that he really admires, and has taken him home, it is a good thing to have his stall [20] in such a part of the establishment that his master shall very often have an eye [21] on the animal; it is well, too, that the stable should be so arranged that the horse's food can no more be stolen out of the manger than his master's out of the storeroom. In my opinion, the man who neglects this matter is neglecting himself; for it is plain that in moments of danger the master gives his own life into the keeping of his horse. A secure stable is a good thing, not only to prevent the stealing of grain, but also because you can easily tell when the horse refuses his feed. Observing this, you may know either that there is too much blood in him, or that he has been overworked and wants rest, or that barley surfeit [22] or some other disease is coming on. In the horse, as in the man, all diseases are easier to cure at the start than after they have become chronic and have been wrongly diagnosed.

The same care which is given to the horse's food and exercise, to make his body grow strong, should also be devoted to keeping his feet in condition. Even naturally sound hoofs get spoiled in stalls with moist, smooth floors. The floors should be sloping, to avoid moisture, and, to prevent smoothness, stones [23] should be sunk close to one another, each about the size of the hoofs. The mere standing on such floors strengthens the feet. Further, of course, the groom should lead the horse out somewhere to rub him down, and should loose him from the manger after breakfast, so that he may go to dinner the more readily. This place outside of the stall would be best suited to the purpose of strengthening the horse's feet if you threw down loosely four or five cartloads of round stones, each big enough to fill your hand and about a pound and a half in weight, surrounding the whole with an iron border to keep them from getting scattered. Standing on these would be as good for him as travelling a stony road for some part of every day; and whether he is being rubbed down or is teased by horseflies, he has to use his hoofs exactly as he does in walking. Stones strewn about in this way strengthen the frogs too. As for his mouth, you must take as much care to make it soft as you take to make his hoofs hard; and the same treatment softens a horse's mouth that softens a man's flesh.[24]

CHAPTER V.

IT is also a horseman's duty, I think, to see that his groom is taught the proper way to treat the horse. First of all, he ought to know that he should never make the knot in the halter at the place where the head-piece fits round. The horse often rubs his head against the manger, and it may make sores if the halter is not easy about the ears; and of course when there are sores, then the horse must be somewhat fretful in bridling and grooming. It is well that the groom should have orders to carry out the droppings and the litter every day to a given place; by doing so he may get rid of it in the easiest way for himself, and would be doing the horse good too. The groom must understand that he is to put the muzzle [25] on the horse when he leads him out to be rubbed down or to the place where he rolls; [26] in fact, the horse ought always to be muzzled whenever he is taken anywhere without a bridle. The muzzle, without hindering his breathing, allows no biting, and when it is on, it serves to keep horses from mischievous designs. The horse should by all means be fastened from above his head; for instinct makes him toss his head up when anything is worrying him about his face, and if he is fastened in this way, the tossing slackens the halter instead of pulling it taut.

In grooming, begin with the head and mane; if the upper parts are not clean, it is waste labour to clean the lower parts. Next raise the hair on the rest of the body by the use of all the ordinary cleaning implements,[27] and then clear away the dust by working with the grain of the hair; but the hair on the backbone should never be touched by any implement at all. It is to be rubbed with the hand, and softly smoothed in its natural direction; for thus the seat would be least injured. The head, however, must be washed with water;[28] it is bony, and to clean it with iron or wood would hurt the horse. The forelock also should be wetted; this hair, even though pretty long, does not prevent the horse from seeing, but clears away from his eyes things that would hurt them. The gods, we must believe, gave this tuft to the horse instead of the huge ears which they gave to asses and mules to protect their eyes.

The tail and mane should be washed, seeing that the hair must be made to grow on the tail, so that the horse, reaching out as far as possible, may switch away things that torment him, and made to grow on the neck to afford plenty to take hold of in mounting. The mane, forelock, and tail are gifts of the gods bestowed on the horse for beauty.[29] A proof is that brood mares, as long as their hair is flowing, are not so apt to admit asses, whence all breeders of mules cut off the hair[30] from their mares preparatory to covering.

CHAPTER V.

Washing down of the legs is a thing I absolutely forbid; it does no good, — on the contrary, daily washing is bad for the hoofs. And washing under the belly should be done very sparingly; it worries the horse more than washing anywhere else, and the cleaner these parts are made, the more they attract things under the belly that would torment it. And no matter what pains one has spent on it, the horse is no sooner led out than it gets exactly as dirty as before. These parts, then, should be let alone; and as for the legs, rubbing with the mere hand is quite enough.

CHAPTER VI.

NEXT I shall explain how a man may groom a horse with the least danger to himself and the greatest good to the animal. If he tries to clean him facing with the horse, he runs the risk of a blow in the face from knee or hoof; but if he faces just the other way and outside the reach of the leg, when he cleans him, and takes his place off the shoulder-blade in rubbing him down, he will not be harmed at all, and may even bend back the hoof and attend to the horse's frog. Let him clean the hind legs in the same way. The man that takes care of the horse should know that both in this matter and in everything else which has to be done, the very last places at which he should approach to do it are in front and behind;

for, if the horse means mischief, these are the two points at which he has the advantage of a man. But by approaching him at the side you can handle him most freely and with the least danger to yourself.

When a horse is to be led, I certainly do not approve of leading him behind you; for then you have the least chance to look out for yourself, and the horse has the best chance to do whatever he likes. Then again I object to teaching the horse to go on ahead with a long leading-rein. The reason is that the horse can then do mischief on either side he pleases, and can even whirl round and face his leader. Why, only think of several horses led together in this fashion, — how in the world could they be kept away from one another? But a horse that is accustomed to be led by the side can do the least mischief to other horses and to men, and would be most convenient and ready for the rider, especially if he should ever have to mount in a hurry.

In order to put the bridle on properly, the groom should first come up on the near [31] side of the horse; then, throwing the reins over the head and letting them drop on the withers, he should take the head-piece [32] in his right hand and offer the bit with his left. If the horse receives it, of course the head-stall [33] is to be put on; but if he does not open his mouth, the bit should be held against his teeth and the thumb of the left hand thrust within his jaw. This makes most horses open the mouth. If he does not receive the bit even then, press his lip hard against the tush; very few horses refuse it on feeling this.

Let your groom be well instructed in the following points: first, never to lead the horse by one rein,[34] for this makes one side of the mouth harder than the other; secondly, what is the proper distance of the bit from the corners of the mouth: if too close, it makes the mouth callous, so that it has no delicacy of feeling; but if the bit hangs too low down in the mouth, the horse can take it in his teeth and so refuse to mind it.

The following must also be urged strongly upon the groom if any work at all is to be done. Willingness to receive the bit is such an important point that a horse which refuses it is utterly useless. Now, if the bridle is put on not only when he is going to be worked, but also when he is led to his food and home after exercise, it would not be at all strange if he should seize the bit of his own accord when you hold it out to him. It is well for the groom to understand how to put a rider up Persian fashion,[35] so that his master, if he gets infirm or has grown oldish, may himself have somebody to mount him handily or may be able to oblige another with a person to mount him.

The one great precept and practice in using a horse is this, — never deal with him when you are in a fit of passion. A fit of passion is a thing that has no foresight in it, and so we often have to rue the day when we gave way to it. Consequently, when your horse shies at an object and is unwilling to go up to it, he should be shown that there is nothing fearful in it, least of all to a courageous horse like him; [36] but if this fails, touch the object yourself that seems so dreadful to him, and lead him up to it with gentleness. Compulsion and blows inspire only the more fear; for when horses are at all hurt at such a time, they think that what they shied at is the cause of the hurt.

I do not find fault with a horse for knowing how to settle down [37] so as to be mounted easily, when the groom delivers him to the rider; still, I think that the true horseman ought to practise and be able to mount even if the horse does not so offer himself. Different horses fall to one's lot at different times, and the same horse serves you one way at one time and another at another.

CHAPTER VII.

I SHALL next set down the method of riding which the horseman may find best for himself and his horse, when once he has received him for mounting. First, then, with the left hand he must take up lightly the halter [38] which hangs from the chin-strap [39] or the noseband, holding it so slack as not to check the horse, whether he intends to raise himself by laying hold of the mane about the ears,[40] and to mount in that way, or whether he vaults on from his spear.[41] With the right hand, he must then take the reins at the withers and also grasp the mane, so that he may not wrench the horse's mouth at all as he gets up. In springing to his place, he must draw up the body with the left hand, keeping his right stiff as he raises himself with it; for in mounting thus, he will not look ungraceful even from behind. The leg should be kept bent, the knee must not touch the horse's back, and the calf must be brought clean over to the off side. After having brought his foot completely round, he is then to settle down in his seat on the horse. I think it good that the horseman should practise springing up from the off side as well, on the chance that he may happen to be leading his horse with the left hand and holding his spear in his right. He has only to learn to do with the left what he did before with the right, and with the right what he did with the left. Another reason why I approve of the latter method of mounting is that the moment he is on horseback the rider would be completely ready, if he should have to engage the enemy all of a sudden.

When the rider takes his seat, whether

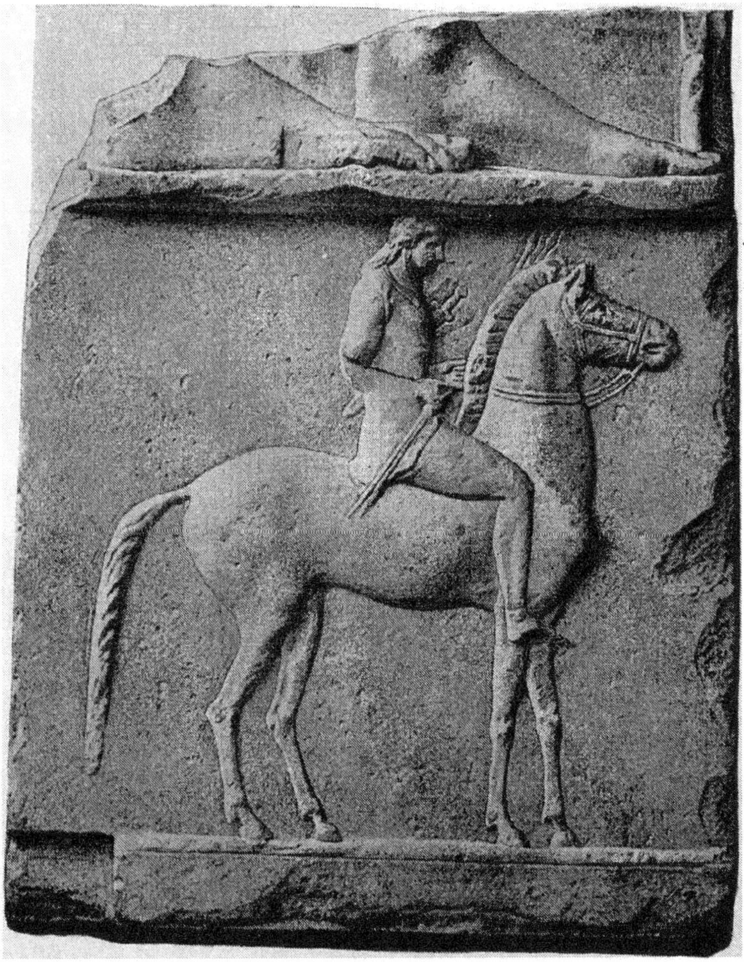

bareback or on the cloth,[42] I do not approve of a seat which is as though the man were on a chair, but rather as though he were standing upright with his legs apart. Thus he would get a better grip with his thighs on the horse, and, being upright, he could hurl his javelin more vigorously and strike a better blow from on horseback, if need be. His foot and leg from the knee down should hang loosely, for if he keeps his leg stiff and should strike it against something, he might get it broken; but a supple leg would yield, if it struck against anything, without at all disturbing the thigh. Then, too, the rider should accustom himself to keep his body above the hips as supple as possible; for this would give him greater power of action, and he would be less liable to a fall if somebody should try to pull or push him off. The horse should be taught to stand still when the rider is taking his seat, and until he has drawn his skirts from under him, if necessary, made the reins even, and taken the most convenient grasp of his spear. Let him then keep his left arm at his side; this will give the rider the tidiest look, and to his hand the greatest power. As for reins, I recommend such as are alike, not weak nor slippery and not thick either, so that if necessary the hand may hold the spear as well.

When the horse gets the signal to start, let him begin at a walk, for this frets him least. If the horse carries his head low, hold the reins with the hands a bit high; if he carries it somewhat high, then rather low: this would make the most graceful appearance. Next, by taking the true trot the horse would relax his body with the least discomfort, and come with the greatest ease into the hand gallop. And as leading with the left is the more approved way, this lead would best be reached if the signal to gallop should be given the horse at the moment when he is rising with his right in the trot; for, being about to raise his left foot next, he would lead with it and would begin the stride as he comes over to the left, — for the horse instinctively leads with the right on turning to the right, and with the left on turning to the left.[43]

I recommend the exercise known as the

Volte, because it accustoms the horse to turn on either jaw. Changing the direction is also a good thing, that the jaws on either side may be equally suppled. But I recommend the Career with sharp turns at each end rather than the complete Volte; for the horse would like turning better after he has had enough of the straight course, and thus would be practising straight-away running and turning at the same time. He must be collected at the turns, because it is not easy or safe for the horse to make short turns when he is at full speed, especially if the ground is uneven or slippery. When the rider collects him, he must not throw the horse aslant at all with the bit, nor sit at all aslant himself; else he must be well aware, that a slight matter will be enough to bring himself and his horse to the ground. The moment the horse faces the stretch after finishing the turn, the rider should push him on to go faster. In war, of course, turns are executed for the purpose of pursuing or retreating; hence it is well that he should be trained to speed after turning.

After the horse appears to have had enough

exercise, it is well to give him a rest and then to urge him suddenly to the top of his speed, either away from other horses or towards them; then to quiet him down out of his speed by pulling him up very short, and again, after a halt, to turn him and push him on. It is very certain that there will come times when each of these manœuvres will be necessary. When the moment comes to dismount, never do so among other horses, nor in a crowd of bystanders, nor outside of the riding-ground; but let the horse enjoy a season of rest in the very place where he is obliged to work.

CHAPTER VIII.

THERE are many occasions, of course, when the horse will have to run down hill and up hill and along a slope, as well as to take a leap across or out of something and to jump down. So all these movements must be learned and practised by both horse and rider. The two will thus become obviously the more helpful and useful to one another. If it is thought that I am repeating myself because I am speaking now of what I have spoken before, let me say that there is no repetition here. I did lay down that you should try whether the horse could do all this at the time you bought him; but what I am now urging is that a man should teach his own horse, and I shall describe the right method of instruction.

With a horse that has no experience whatever in leaping, take him with the leading rein loose and leap across the ditch before him; then draw the rein tight to make him jump over. If he refuses, let somebody with a whip or stick lay it on pretty hard; he will then jump over not merely the proper distance but a great deal more than is required. He will never need a blow after that, but will jump the minute he sees anybody coming up behind him. When he is used to taking a leap in this way, let the rider mount and put him first at small and then at larger ditches, pricking him with the spur[44] just as he is about to leap. Prick him with the spur in the same way in teaching him to leap up and to leap down. If the horse uses his whole body at once for all these, it will be much safer for him and for his rider than if his quarters are not well gathered in as he leaps or jumps up or down.

Going down hill must be taught him at first on soft ground, and finally, when he gets used to it, he will like to run down much more than to run up. As for the fears that some folks feel of dislocating the horse's shoulders in riding down hill, they should take courage from the knowledge that the horses of the Persians and Odrysians,[45] all of whom habitually run their races down hill, are not a bit less sound than Greek horses.

I shall not omit to tell how the rider himself ought to conform to all these movements. When the horse bolts suddenly off, the rider should lean forward, for then the horse would be less likely to draw in under the rider and jolt him up; but he should bend back when the horse is being brought to a poise, as he would then be less jolted. In leaping a ditch or running up hill, it is not a bad thing to lay hold of the mane,[46] so that the horse may not be troubled by the bit and the ground at the same time. Going down a steep place, the rider should throw himself well back, and support the horse by the bit, so that rider and horse may not be carried headlong down the hill.

It is well that the rides should be in different directions occasionally, and that they should be sometimes long and sometimes short. The horse is apt to dislike [47] this less than riding always in the same places and over the same distance. The rider must have a firm seat when going at full speed over all sorts of ground, and must also be able to use his weapons well on horseback. Hence there is nothing to be said against the practice of riding in the hunt, where there is a suitable country with wild animals; [48] but where these are not to be had, it is good training for two riders to arrange together, one to fly from the other on horseback over all sorts of ground, wheeling about with his spear and retreating again, while the other pursues with buttons on his javelins and on his spear. Whenever he gets within javelin-shot, he is to hurl his button-tipped javelins at the runner, and to strike him with his spear when he overtakes him within striking distance. If they come to close quarters, it is well for one to pull his adversary towards him and then to thrust him back all of a sudden; this is the way to unhorse him. But the proper thing for the man who is being pulled to do, is to urge his horse forward; for by so doing, he will be more likely to unhorse the other man than to get a fall himself.

And if ever there is cavalry skirmishing, when two armies are set in array against each other, and the one side pursues even to the enemy's main body, while the other retreats among its friends, it is well just here to bear in mind that while one is among his friends he is both brave and safe in wheeling among the first and pressing on at full speed, but that when he gets near the foe he should keep his horse well in hand; for thus, while doing hurt to the enemy, he could probably best escape being hurt by them himself.

The gods have bestowed upon man the gift of teaching his brother man what he ought to do by word of mouth; but it is evident that by word of mouth you can teach a horse nothing. If, however, you reward him with kindness after he has done as you wish, and punish him when he disobeys, he will be most likely to learn to obey as he ought. This rule, to be sure, may be expressed in a few words, but it holds good in every branch of the art of horsemanship. For instance, he would receive the bit the more readily if some good should come of it every time he received it; and he will leap and jump up and obey in all the rest if he looks forward to a season of rest on finishing what he has been directed to do.

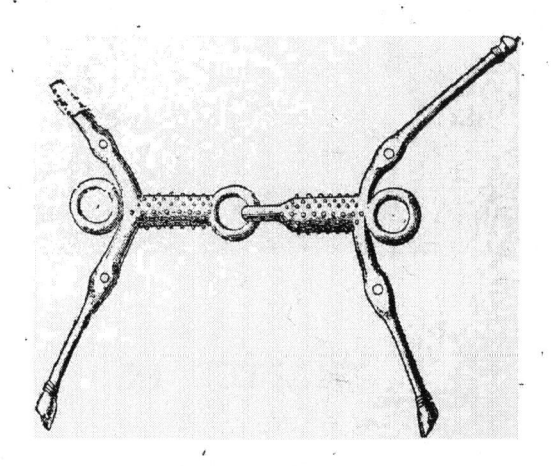

CHAPTER IX.

SO far, then, it has been stated how a person would be least likely to be cheated in buying a colt or a horse, and least likely to spoil him in use, but particularly how one could produce a horse with all the qualities that a rider needs in war. Now, on the chance that you should happen to have a horse that is either too high-mettled for the occasion or too sluggish, this is perhaps the proper time to set down how to treat either one in the most correct fashion. In the first place you are to know that mettle is to a horse what temper is to a man. Exactly, therefore, as a man who neither says nor does anything harsh would be least likely to rouse the temper of his neighbour, so one who avoids fretting a high-mettled horse would be the last to exasperate him. At the very outset, then, in mounting, care should be taken to mount without annoying him. After mounting, the rider should sit quiet more than the ordinary time, and then move him forward by the most gentle signs possible. Next, beginning very slowly, induce him in turn to quicker paces in such a way that the horse may reach full speed almost without knowing it. Every abrupt sign that you make him — sudden sights, sounds, or impressions — all disturb a high-mettled horse just as they do a man. [Abruptness, you must remember, always confuses a horse.[49]] If you want to collect a high-mettled horse when he is dashing along faster than is convenient, you should not draw rein abruptly, but should win him over gently with the bit, calming him down and not forcing him to be still. Long stretches, rather than frequent turns, calm horses down, and leisurely riding for a good while soothes, calms down, and does not rouse the spirit of the horse of mettle. But if anybody expects to calm such a horse down by tiring him out with riding swiftly and far, his supposition is just the reverse of the truth; these are exactly the circumstances in which the high-mettled horse tries to carry the day by main force, and in his wrath, like an angry man, he often does much irreparable harm to himself and his rider. A high-mettled horse must be kept from dashing on at full speed, and utterly prevented from racing with another; for, as a rule, remember, the most ambitious horses are the highest-mettled.

Smooth bits [50] are more suitable for such horses than rough; but if a rough one is put in, it must be made as easy as the smooth by lightness of hand. It is well also to get into the habit of sitting quiet, especially on a high-mettled horse, and utterly to avoid touching him with any other part than those which we use in securing a firm seat. You must know that it is orthodox to calm him down with a chirrup[51] and to rouse him by clucking; still, if from the first you should cluck when caressing and chirrup when punishing, the horse would learn to start up at the chirrup and calm down at a cluck. So when a shout is raised or a trumpet blown, you should not let him see you disturbed, least of all should you do anything to alarm him, but should quiet him down so far as you can at such a time, and give him his breakfast or his dinner if circumstances should permit. But the best piece of advice I can give is not to get a very high-mettled horse to use in war.

As for a sluggish horse, I think it sufficient to set down that your method of handling him should at all times be just the opposite to that which I recommended in the case of the high-mettled one.[52]

CHAPTER X.

IF you desire to handle a good war-horse so as to make his action the more magnificent and striking, you must refrain from pulling at his mouth with the bit as well as from spurring and whipping him. Most people think that this is the way to make him look fine; but they only produce an effect exactly contrary to what they desire,— they positively blind their horses by jerking the mouth up instead of letting them look forward, and by spurring and striking scare them into disorder and danger. This is the way horses behave that are fretted by their riders into ugly and ungraceful action; but if you teach your horse to go with a light hand on the bit, and yet to hold his head well up and to arch his neck, you will be making him do just what the animal himself glories and delights in. A proof that he really delights in it is that when a horse is turned loose and runs off to join other horses, and especially towards mares, then he holds his head up as high as he can, arches his neck in the most spirited style, lifts his legs with free action, and raises his tail. So when he is induced by a man to assume all the airs and graces which he puts on of himself when he is showing off voluntarily, the result is a horse that likes to be ridden, that presents a magnificent sight, that looks alert, that is the observed of all observers. I shall now attempt to explain how I think this result may be obtained.

In the first place you must own at least two bits.[53] Let one of them be smooth, with the discs on it good-sized; the other with the discs heavy, and not standing so high, but with the *echini* sharp, so that,

CHAPTER X. 57

when he seizes it, he may drop it from dislike of its roughness. Then, when he shall have received the smooth bit in its turn, he will like its smoothness and do everything on the smooth bit which he has been trained to do on the rough. He may, however, come not to mind its smoothness and to bear hard upon it; and this is why we put the large discs on the smooth bit, to make him keep his jaws apart and drop the bit. You can make the rough bit anything you like by holding it lightly or drawing it tight.

No matter what the kind of bit, it must always be flexible. When a horse seizes a stiff bit, he holds the whole of it at once against his bars; he lifts it all, just as a man does a spit, at whatever point he takes it up. But the other kind acts like a chain; only the part that you are grasping remains unbending, and the rest hangs loose. So, as the horse is always after the part that is getting away from him in his mouth, he drops the bit from his bars. For the same reason little rings are hung from the joints of the bit in the middle, so that the horse, in trying to catch them with his tongue and teeth, may not think of snatching up the bit against his bars.[54]

I will set down the definitions of flexible and stiff bits, in case some reader may not know them. The bit is flexible when the joints are broad and smooth where they meet, so that it bends easily; and all the pieces put on round the joints are more likely to be flexible if they are roomy and not tight. On the contrary, if the different parts of the bit do not run and play into each other easily, the bit is a stiff one.

Whatever the kind of bit, it must be used according to the following rules, which are in every case the same, provided that it is desired to give a horse the look that has been described. The horse's mouth must not be checked too harshly, so that he will toss his head, nor too gently for him to feel it. The moment he acknowledges it and begins to raise his neck, give him the bit. And in everything else, as I have insisted over and over again, the horse should be rewarded as long as he behaves well. When you see a horse show his pleasure by carrying his neck high and yielding to the hand, there is no

CHAPTER X.

need of using harsh measures, as though you were forcing him to work; he should rather be coaxed on, as when you wish him to rest. He will then go forward most cheerfully to his swift paces. A proof that the horse enjoys fast running is that when he has got loose he never moves at a walk, but runs. It is his nature to enjoy it, unless he is obliged to run an excessive distance. Neither horse nor man likes anything in the world that is excessive.

When it comes to his riding in a proud and stately style, — in the first part of his training we accustomed him, you remember, to dash forward at full speed after making the turns. Well, after he has learned this, if you support him by the bit and at the same moment give him one of the signs to dash forward, the bit holds him in and the signal to advance rouses him up. He will then throw out his chest and raise his legs rather high, and furiously though not flexibly; for horses do not use their legs very flexibly when they are being hurt. Now if, when his fire is thus kindled, you let him have the bit, the slackness of it makes him think that he is given his head, and in his joy thereat he will bound along with proud gait and prancing legs, imitating exactly the airs that he puts on before other horses. Everybody that sees such a horse cries out that he is free, willing, fit to ride, high-mettled, brilliant, and at once beautiful and fiery in appearance.

So much for this subject, in case you are an admirer of such action.

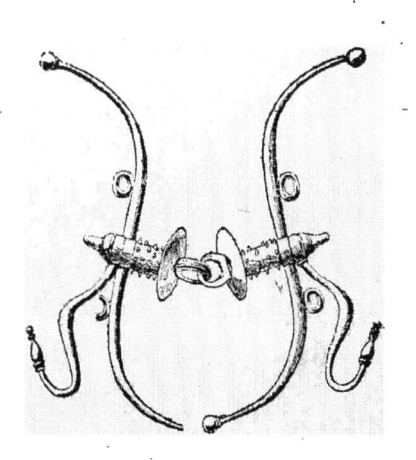

CHAPTER XI.

IF you chance to wish to own a horse for parade,[55] a high-stepper and of showy action, such qualities are not, as a rule, to be found in every horse, but he must have, to start with, the natural gifts of high spirit and strong body. Some people fancy that if a horse has supple legs, it follows that he will be able to rear his body on them; but this is not the fact. It is the horse with supple loins, and short and strong ones too, that can do this. I do not mean the loins at the tail, but at the belly, between the ribs and the haunches. Such a horse will be able to gather the hind legs well in under the fore.[56] Now when he has gathered them well in, if you take him up with the bit, he falls back on his hocks and raises his forehand so that his belly and sheath can be seen from the front. You must give him the bit when he does this, and it will look to the spectators as if he were doing all of his own accord the prettiest feat that a horse can do. There are, to be sure, some persons who teach this movement either by tapping the hocks with a rod, or by directing somebody to run along by the side and strike him with a stick under the gaskins. But for my part, I think, as I have said all along, that it is the best of lessons if the horse gets a season of repose whenever he has behaved to his rider's satisfaction.

For what the horse does under compulsion, as Simon also observes, is done without understanding; and there is no beauty in it either, any more than if one should whip and spur a dancer. There would be a great deal more ungracefulness than beauty in either a horse or a man that was so treated. No, he should show off all his finest and most brilliant performances willingly and at a mere sign. If he goes on at his exercise till he is covered with sweat, and then if you dismount and unbridle him the moment he rears up in fine style, you must be sure that he will come to the act of rearing with a will. This is the attitude in which the horses of gods and heroes are always depicted, and men who can handle a horse gracefully in it are a magnificent sight. The horse rearing thus is such a thing of wonder as to fix the eyes of all beholders, young or old. Nobody, I assure you, either leaves him or gets tired of watching him as long as he presents the brilliant spectacle.

Yet if it chance that the owner of such a horse should command a troop [57] or regiment of cavalry, he should not aspire to be the only brilliant figure himself, but should try all the more to make the whole line that follows a sight worth seeing. If he goes on ahead at an extremely slow pace, with his horse rearing very high and very often, it is obvious that the rest of the horses would have to follow him at a walk. What could there be at all brilliant in such a sight as this? But if you rouse your horse and take the lead at a gait neither too fast nor too slow, but simply suited to the horses that are most spirited, alert, and graceful in action, with such leading the general effect is complete, and the horses prance and snort all together, so that not only you yourself but all that follow after would be a sight well worth seeing.[58]

To conclude, if a man buys his horses skilfully, feeds them so that they can bear fatigue, and handles them properly in training them for war, in exercising them for the parade and in actual service in the field, what is there to prevent him from making his horses more valuable than when he acquired them, and hence from owning horses that are famous and from becoming famous himself in the art of horsemanship? Nothing except the interposition of some divinity.

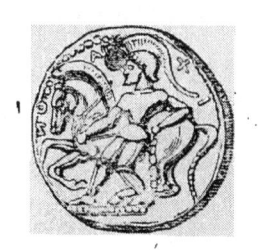

CHAPTER XII.

I WISH also to set down how the man who is to run the hazard of battle on horseback should be armed. To begin with the cuirass.[59] This must always be made to fit the body; for if it fits well, the body supports its weight, but if it is very loose, the shoulders have to carry it all by themselves. As for too tight a cuirass, it is a straitjacket and not a piece of armour. Next, as the neck is one of the vital parts, I say that a covering should be made for it rising out of the cuirass itself to fit the neck.[60] This will at once be an ornament; and if it is made as it should be, it will cover the rider's face when he pleases as far as the nose. For a helmet the Boeotian [61] is the best, in my opinion, since it most completely protects all the parts that are above the cuirass, without preventing you from seeing. Let the cuirass be made so as not to hinder sitting nor stooping. Round the belly, the groin, and thereabouts, there should be flaps of such material and number as to protect these parts. Since the horseman is disabled if anything happens to his left arm, I consequently recommend the newly invented piece of armour called *the arm*.[62] It protects the shoulder, the arm, the elbow, and the part that holds the reins, and it can be extended or bent together; besides it covers the gap left by the cuirass under the armpit.

The right arm must of course be raised whenever the rider wants to hurl his javelin or to strike a blow. The part of the cuirass that hinders this must therefore be removed, and in its place flaps put on at the joints, unfolding all together when the arm is raised and closing when it is lowered. For the arm itself, something worn like a greave [63] seems to me better than to have it of a piece with

CHAPTER XII. 67

the cuirass. The part of the arm that is bared when it is raised [64] must be protected near the cuirass with calfskin or bronze, else it will be left unguarded in its most vital part.

Now, as the rider himself is in extreme danger if anything happens to his horse, the animal also should be armed with a frontlet, breastplate, and thigh-pieces; [65] the last serve at the same time to cover the thighs of the rider. Above all, the horse's belly should be protected, as being the most vital and the weakest part. It may be protected with the cloth. This cloth [66] must also be of such material and so sewed together as to give the rider a safe seat and not to gall the horse's back. For the rest, this should be the armour for horse and man; but as the shins and feet would of course project below the thigh-pieces, they too may be armed with top-boots [67] of the leather of which shoes are made. These will at once protect the shins and cover the feet.

This and the grace of the gods is the defensive armour. For offensive, I recommend the sabre [68] rather than the sword; for the rider being aloft, a scimitar blow will be more in place than the thrust of a sword. Instead of a spear of scantling, which is weak and clumsy to carry, I am inclined to recommend two javelins[69] made of cornel wood. A skilful person can throw one and then use the other in front, on the flank, or in the rear. They are also stronger than the spear and handier to carry.

I recommend hurling the javelin at the longest possible range. This gives more time to recover oneself and to seize the other javelin. I will set down in a few words the best method of hurling the javelin. Throw forward the left, draw back the right, rise from the thighs, and let it go with the point slightly raised. Then it will carry with the greatest force and the longest range, and it will be sure to hit the mark, provided the point is always aimed at the mark when you let it go.

This completes the hints, lessons, and exercises on which I was to write for the private. The knowledge and practice necessary for the commander of cavalry have been set forth already in a different work.[70]

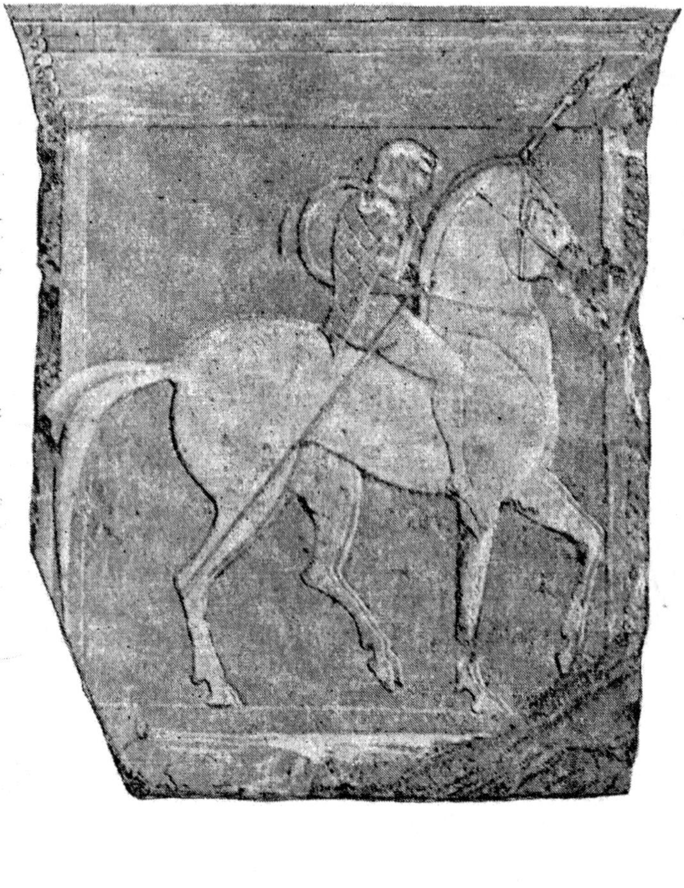

THE GREEK RIDING-HORSE.

XENOPHON'S "Treatise on Horsemanship" is the oldest extant work on the subject in any language, and the only one which has come down to us in either Greek or Latin. That the author was well entitled to begin it as he does, will be granted by every reader of his masterpiece, the Anabasis. But though in the ill-fated expedition which that book describes, he travelled nearly three thousand miles, generally on horseback, yet this journey occupied only a little more than a year of his life; and probably before the expedition, and certainly after it, he saw service in the cavalry.

We know very little of the life of Xenophon before the year 401 B. C., in which he joined the army of Cyrus. He was an Athenian, and from a very early age was the follower and friend of Socrates. Whether at the time of the Anabasis he was forty years old or only a little over thirty, is a question which not all the wisdom of the learned has yet been able to settle. After the disastrous failure of Cyrus's enterprise, it was Xenophon, until then a mere honorary staff-officer, who aroused his companions from their dejection; the remainder of the Anabasis tells the story how his courage and skill brought them back to Greek lands from among the Persians. But his success was not appreciated at Athens, and he was banished for serving with Spartans and against the Persians, with whom the Athenians had latterly allied themselves. Becoming again a soldier of fortune, he joined the king of Sparta, Agesilaus, and followed him against Athens and Thebes in the battle of Coronea, 394 B. C. For his services the Spartans presented him with an estate at Scillus in Elis, about 387 B.C.; and there he lived for more than fifteen years, with his wife Philesia and their sons Gryllus and Diodorus. In this retirement were produced several of his well-known works. After the battle of Leuctra, in 371, he was driven out of Scillus and went to Corinth. Some tell us that the Athenians recalled him from exile, and that his last years were spent in his native city; others say that he died in Corinth. It is certain that his sons, at least, were in the service of Athens in the campaign which closed with Mantinea in 362. Not long before this battle he wrote "The General of Horse," as we know from allusions in it to the approaching hostilities. This book, in turn, is referred to in the treatise on Horsemanship, which must have shortly followed; and one likes to believe that both were designed by the old soldier to serve for the guidance of his sons. The labor of love, if such it was, failed not of reward. The sons were worthy of their father, and for their courage and manly beauty won the title of the Dioscuri, the "Great Twin Brethren." The elder, Gryllus, crowned his life by falling gloriously at Mantinea. "And there came one to Xenophon as he was offering sacrifice, and said, 'Gryllus is dead.' And Xenophon took off the garland that was on his head, but ceased not his sacrifice. Then the messenger said, 'His death was noble.' And Xenophon returned the garland to his head again; and it is in the tale that he shed no tears, but said, 'I knew that I begat him mortal.'" So runs the story; and it is added that Diodorus came safely out of the battle, and lived to rear a son of his brother's name. Xenophon himself died at a good old age, not later than 355.

There is no reason for doubting the tradition that Xenophon's family belonged to the Equestrian* class in the state, and that consequently he served in the cavalry in his youth. He was old enough to have borne a man's part in the last years of the Peloponnesian War and during the episode of the Thirty Tyrants; but history does not even mention his name in connection with either. Still, his whole bearing during the retreat of the Ten Thousand was far from being that of a mere

* See p. 75.

tiro in military affairs, and it is safe to assume that he had already seen service in the Athenian cavalry. Even after the battle of Coronea he still had opportunities for keeping up his acquaintance with horses. He was always as far as possible from being a closet scholar; and no man not a lover of the free, vigorous outdoor life of the country could write, as Xenophon does in the "Oeconomicus," with such a particular acquaintance with all the various sides of a country gentleman's life. The preparation of the soil for all its different products, the tilling and sowing, and then the reaping, threshing, and winnowing of the grain, the planting and tending of trees and flowers, the care of that all-important olive which entered into so many of the relations of Greek life, — all these were familiar to him, and the oversight of the farm-labourers and bailiffs as well. Nor did he neglect field-sports. Once a year there was a grand hunt on his estate to which all the country round was invited; and his treatise on Hunting, with its full account of the breeding and the training of dogs, shows that the annual hunt was by no means the only one in which he took part. Surely these pursuits called for horse-raising, horse-training, and horse-riding; and that he became a master in each, the treatise on Horsemanship is evidence enough.

This treatise is confined to the horse that is to be ridden, not driven; and the remarks which follow will therefore be limited in the same way. Riding, as a habit, seems to have come into practice later than driving; at least, this is true of the Greeks. A few passages in Homer are often quoted to show that even in the Heroic Age men sometimes used horses for riding; but this interpretation of the passages is a mistake, and the whole general tone of Epic poetry proves that driving was the common practice.[71] In battle, cavalry was utterly unknown. The heroes fought in chariots, the mass of the army on foot; and journeys, even over mountainous country, were made in chariots.

But in the course of the following centuries there came about a change. We cannot trace its development; but it is a fact that in the Olympic games, in which originally the only equestrian contests were chariot races, there was instituted a race for full-grown riding-horses as early as the thirty-third Olympiad (648 B. C.). In battle the chariot had disappeared even before the Persian wars, but its place was not filled by cavalry until after them. The Athenians had no cavalry at Marathon; and although we know that wealthy citizens kept horses, it is probable that they were bred for racing. Doubtless it was acquaintance with the Persian cavalry that led to the organization of a body of horse at Athens. From the first and throughout its history, it was a *corps d'élite*, selected from the second highest class of citizens in order of wealth. The whole body consisted of only a thousand men, one hundred from each of the ten Attic tribes; each hundred was commanded by a *phylarch*, and the entire corps by two *hipparchs*. It was under the especial oversight of the Senate; entrance into it, while enforced upon the physically and pecuniarily able, was governed by a strict examination, and the horseman was required to present himself before an examining committee,* with his charger, and his equipments, all in a condition to conform to the law. In spite of their care, however, the Greeks never accomplished the revolution in military art which gave cavalry a decisive rôle in action. This was reserved for the Macedonians. Greek cavalry was used, as a rule, only to harass a marching enemy, or to follow up and complete a victory already won; and probably horsemen seldom went nearer than within javelin shot of a body of infantry in line of battle.

That only the rich could serve in this arm is evident from the facts that each man had to supply his own horse, and that horses were very expensive animals. A very ordinary horse cost three minae, or sixty-four dollars; a fine animal, such as would be used in war or for racing, much more. Thus we hear of what might be called a thoroughbred as costing twelve minae,[72] one hundred and eighty-six dollars. Xenophon paid a little less than this for a war-horse which he bought in Lampsacus. Such prices for fine horses

---

* See the accompanying illustration, and its description on page 163.

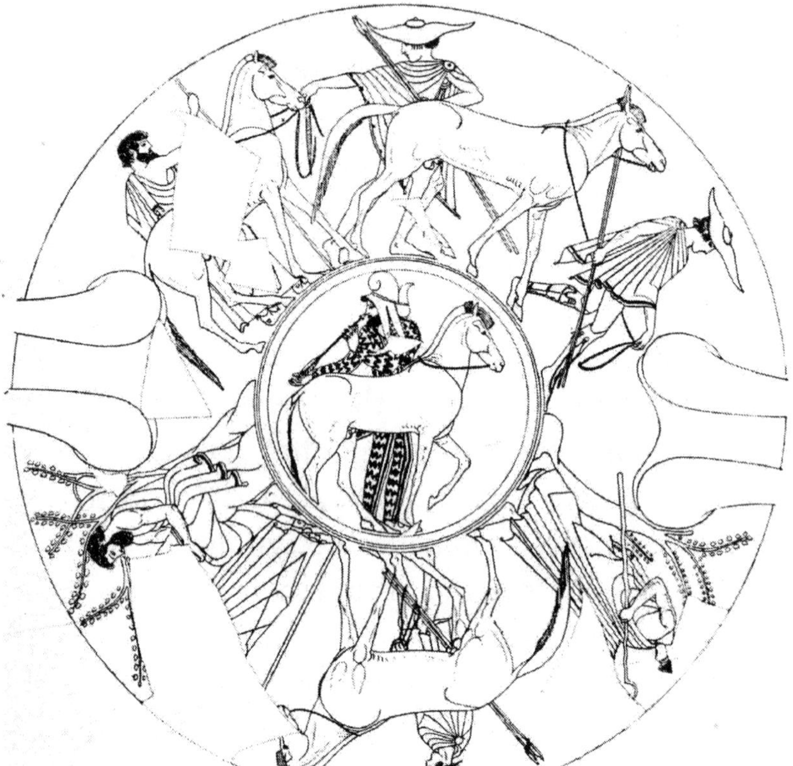

seem low to us; but it should be remembered that the cheapness of a given article is relative to the cost of other articles at the time in question. In Greek antiquity, the necessaries of life were in general to be bought for comparatively less money than at the present day. A house cost from three to one hundred and twenty minae ($54 to $2,160), according to its size, situation, and condition; perhaps an average price was from ten to forty minae ($180 to $720). Barley cost two drachmae the *medimnus* (thirty-six cents for a bushel and a half); wheat, three drachmae (fifty-four cents). An ox could be had for from fifty to one hundred drachmae (nine to eighteen dollars); a sheep, for ten to twenty drachmae; a sucking pig, for three drachmae; a lamb, for ten drachmae. For the usual garment of the working classes the same price was paid as for a lamb ($1.80); for a cloak, such as cavalrymen wore, twelve drachmae ($2.16). These prices are gleaned by Boeckh[*] here and there throughout the literature. A comparison of them makes it evident that a horse was an expensive piece

[*] In "Die Staatshaushaltung der Athener."

of property; and indeed horse-owning, with all that was too apt to follow it, became a synonym for extravagance.

Horse-raising was a pursuit for which the nature of the Greek soil was not well fitted; the countries were too rugged and mountainous, the plains in them few and small. Chief among the breeds for beauty, courage, and endurance was the Thessalian. It was renowned in the very earliest times, but then of course for driving and not for riding. The mares of King Diomedes which ate human flesh, the horses of Rhesus, of Achilles, and of Orestes in the race described by Sophocles in the "Electra,"— finally, to come down from mythology to history, Alexander's charger, Bucephalas, were all of this famous breed. Others in high favour were the Argive, Acarnanian, Arcadian, and Epidaurian; but nothing is known of the differences between these breeds or of the peculiar merits of each.

In spite of the natural disadvantages of the soil of Attica, the Athenian young men devoted themselves with much zeal to the raising and training of horses for the turf or for war; and old Strepsiades * was not the only father who had to lament that he was ruined by a horse-complaint. The great space devoted on the frieze of the Parthenon to the Athenian cavalry shows clearly what a high estimation was set upon the possession of beautiful horses, and on dexterity in the management of them. Instruction in riding began to form a special branch in the education of the higher classes,† and it was therefore natural that men should begin to write on the art of horsemanship.

The celebrated rider Simon, of whom more hereafter, was the earliest writer on this art whose name is known to us. He was soon followed by Xenophon. From the latter's treatise we can discover the point which the art had reached in the first half of the fourth century before the Christian era. We learn from it that the only gaits of the horse were the walk, the trot, and the gallop with both leads; that he was trained in leaping as well as in the demi-pesade, the volte, and the oblong career with sharp turns at both ends;

* In the comedy of the "Clouds" by Aristophanes.
† See page 169.

that the use of the jointed bit and of the spur was understood; but that curbs, saddles, and stirrups were not yet invented. We get also much information on the nature of the ani mal himself, and on the care that was taken of him. I have found it more convenient to say what seemed necessary on all these matters in the notes which follow this essay. But Xenophon's first chapter is devoted to the physique of the animal; and in it he sets forth what, in his opinion, are the distinguishing marks of a good horse. This is a subject which may be better treated here than in the notes.

In the matter of judging the points of a horse, the ancient requirements were not in all respects like the modern. The advance in anatomical knowledge accounts for some differences; but it is also probable, as Schlieben* observes, that we, like the men of old, are prejudiced by habit in favour of the type with which we are familiar. If qualities which they thought beautiful seem ugly to us, it should be remembered that our standard does not always conform even to that of the last century.

* In "Die Pferde des Altertums."

Our knowledge of the taste of the Greeks in this matter is drawn from two sources, — the literary and the artistic. Schlieben, in his interesting book on the Horse in Antiquity, seems to think that the three principal forms of art — vase-paintings, reliefs, and statues in the round — each exhibit peculiarities of treatment innate to the artistic form, which make it impossible to reach, from a comparison of them all, any distinct conception of the best type of Greek horse. Then turning to the writers, he is further confused by finding that points of excellence upon which they all agree are not apparent in the works of the artists. Hence he assumes different ideals for the artists and the writers. He even thinks that in one point, at least, the unanimous agreement of the writers is reversed by as complete a contrary agreement in works of art. This point is the mane. He makes the common errors of believing that all the artists represent it as short, and that all the writers say that it should be long. Neither belief is more than an assumption, and a baseless one at that, as will appear later. The fact is, Schlieben seems to expect to find in the works of all sorts of artists, good, bad, and indifferent, the same consensus that really is to be found in the writings of the authors. But the works of art have survived to us from different centuries by means of all kinds of accidents, and they were produced for all kinds of reasons. The books have survived, generally, for the reason that they were fittest for survival. The authors lived, none of them, before the classical period, and each of them undertook to describe a horse because he knew the animal himself, and had spent a good part of his life with horses, or because he could copy the words of authors of more practical experience than his own. There can be no question of the vast advantage of the books over the works of art in deciding such a matter as this.

There would be nothing very surprising, therefore, in the want of agreement in art, if such want there be, upon a type of horse which we can take for the ideal animal. But nobody should thence proceed to argue that there was no such type already determined by judges of horseflesh and agreed upon even by artists. It would be much more

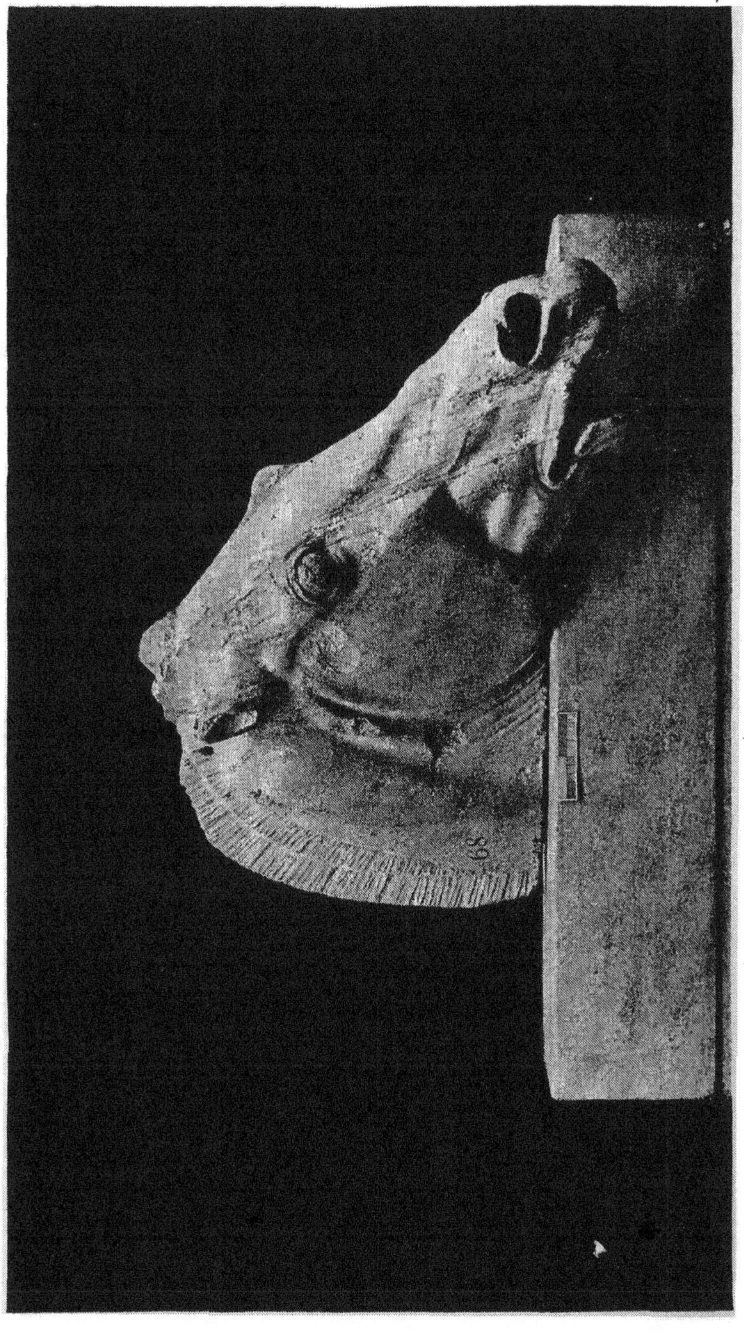

THE GREEK RIDING-HORSE. 83

likely that it was the want of technical skill which prevented the artist from representing what he had in mind to represent; then, too, he might be fettered by convention. When we look at a picture on an archaic vase, we are standing at the very cradle of the art of painting,— in order of time the last of the fine arts which the Greeks developed. And we see on vases of the more cultivated period many things which illustrate the power which lies in methods sanctified by custom — that is, in convention — to over-ride the real knowledge of the art of painting and the greater perfection of technique which existed at the time of the production of such works. In criticising an equestrian statue or a relief for a frieze, one should always remember that it was intended to be placed at a considerable elevation and to be looked at from below, so that exaggeration of certain parts was often necessary, — such, for instance, as in the treatment of the eyes of the famous horse's head by Phidias[*] in the eastern pediment of the Parthenon. But when all allowances are made, a perfect horse is as rare a thing in

[*] See the opposite cut.

Greek art as he is in nature. Even on the Parthenon frieze, where there are finer horses than in any other works of Greek art, some animals have faults which are apparent to the veriest tiro. In fact, if we should judge altogether by what has survived to us, it must be admitted that in representing the horse in all the different forms of art the ancients have been surpassed by modern artists. By Phidias we have only the heads that were in the pediments; for the figures on the frieze, although designed by him, were certainly not carved by his own hand. But Phidias stood alone, and far above contemporaries and successors. Still, in spite of the fact that many ancient representations of the horse have no claim to beauty or to correctness in composition, there are others which will better bear criticism, some deserve high praise, and we read of artists who won great fame in antiquity for the realism with which they depicted the animal. Apelles, to whom Philip and Alexander often sat for their likenesses, is said to have painted a horse [73] with such truth to nature that a live horse neighed at the picture! Pauson was commissioned to paint a horse rolling,* but he painted him running with a cloud of dust about him. The man who gave the order naturally objected, whereupon the master turned the picture upside down, and behold! the patron's stipulations were fulfilled.[74] Criticism could discover only one defect in a painting by Micon; the famous rider Simon remarked that he had never before seen a horse with eyelashes on the lower lids.[75] Such stories, in spite of manifest exaggerations, show that extant works are not a fair criterion of the skill of the great painters Not a single work remains that can be traced to any of them; but doubtless to their art, in comparison with what survives, might have been applied lines like Donne's, written of a contemporary of his own,—

> "A hand or eye
> By Hilyarde drawne, is worth an history
> By a worse painter made."

In sculpture, both in the round and in relief, and in reliefs on coins, the extant works are far more satisfactory; for they rep-

* See p. 131.

resent branches of art which had reached near to perfection before the Greeks really began to develop painting. But here again, as I have said, we lack complete examples of works illustrating the horse by the greatest masters, except perhaps by the best designers for the coinage. On the whole, it seems impossible, from a comparison of the works of art alone, to determine what shape of horse was generally approved by the Greek connoisseur. It remains to inquire whether the literature helps us in this direction.

The oldest known description in Greek of a good horse was contained in Simon's treatise on Horsemanship, of which we have only fragments. One, however, is of considerable length, and this happens to contain his advice on the choice of a horse. Then comes Xenophon; but after him we find nothing professing exactness until the Roman period. Varro, writing in 37 B. C., and Vergil, who published his "Georgics" a little later, are the only others before the Christian era. Then come in the first century Calpurnius and Columella, in the third Oppian and Nemesian, and in the fourth Apsyrtus, Pelagonius, and Palladius.[76] There are of course countless allusions to the points of the horse in numerous other authors, but I have here named all the extant writers who have described with any exactness and completeness the best type of the animal; and in another part of this book (p. 107) will be found translations which I have made from them all.

These writers are scattered through a period of nearly eight hundred years, but it is evident that they all had in mind an animal of the same general stamp. Schlieben writes as though the descriptions given by the several writers really differed in essential particulars; but this is very far from being the case, and his study of the passages cannot have been exact. Xenophon's description is by all odds the most complete; in his first chapter he touches upon over thirty points, many more than are mentioned by any other writer. A careful examination of them all shows that there are only five points mentioned by others but omitted by him; namely, shoulder-blades (large, Simon and Apsyrtus; broad, Varro; strong, Nemesian); teeth (small,

Simon); gaskins (not fleshy, Simon); veins (visible all over the body, Varro); coronet, (moderate, Pelagonius). On the other hand, the other writers never disagree with Xenophon in the points which they do mention. The only approach to such disagreement is the long barrel apparently required by both Simon and by Palladius; but Xenophon was speaking only of riding-horses, while there is nothing to show that these writers had not also in mind horses for driving. It is true that we find some additions to Xenophon's descriptions of certain points; but these are only additions and not contradictions, and he would doubtless have agreed with most of them. Such, for instance, are the muscles bulging out all over the chest (Vergil, Columella, Apsyrtus, Palladius), the jaw brought close to the neck (Simon, Oppian), the straight cannons (Columella, Oppian). It appears, then, that there is a very close agreement among the different writers; further, the resemblance in their language and the order in which they take up the various points show that they were frequently copying from one another or from

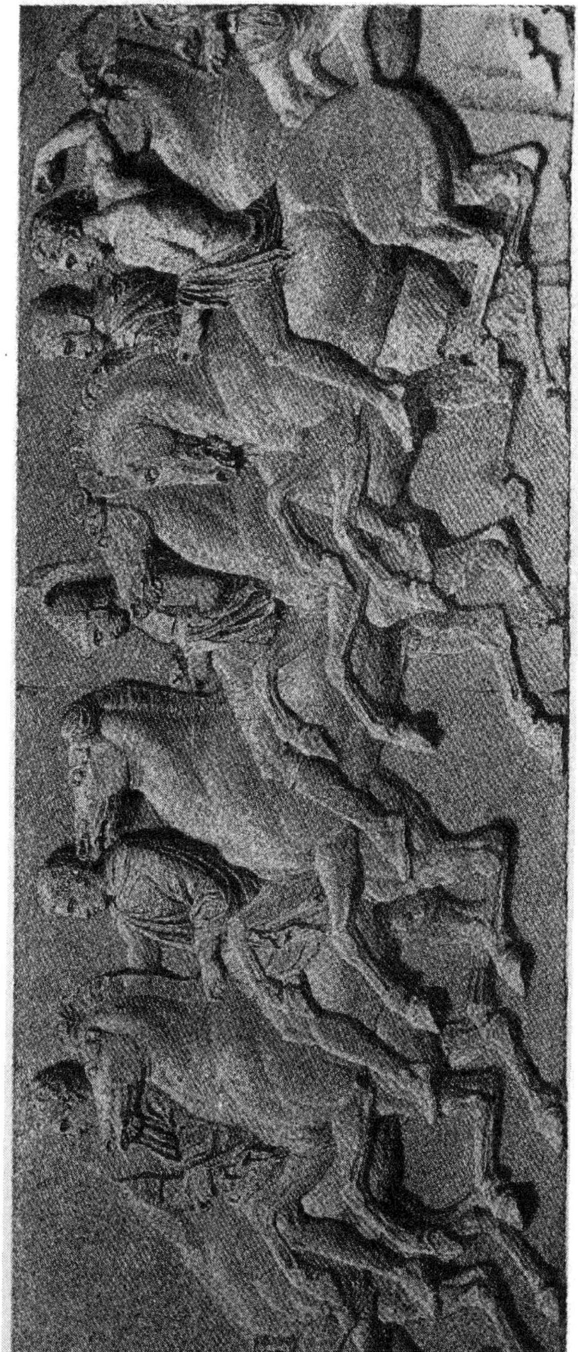

a common source now lost to us.* There can be little doubt, therefore, that even before Xenophon's time an ideal or normal type had been established which was to find acceptance throughout the whole period of Greek and Roman antiquity.

Now, when we compare Xenophon's description of a good horse with the best horses on the frieze of the Parthenon, we find a remarkable similarity. In fact, as "Stonehenge" † remarks, "here we have described a cobby but spirited and corky horse, with a light and somewhat peculiar carriage of the head and neck, just as we see represented on the Elgin marbles." It has been thought by some that Xenophon based his description upon these very reliefs, and it is of course possible that they may have served as a sort of guide to his words. But from earlier works still, in vase-paintings of extremely

* A lost work by the elder Pliny contained a description of the normal horse, generally accepted by his contemporaries. See his Natural History, viii, 162.

† In his book on the Horse, near the beginning of which he gives the most exact translation of Xenophon's description which I have ever seen

rude workmanship, presenting pictures which to the Philistine are nothing but ridiculous caricatures, — even in these early productions and still more frequently on the later vases, there are traces which show that it was the artist's hand that was at fault, or that he was governed by convention, and that there was present before his mind something very like the conception which the assistants of Phidias were enabled to work out, — some of them, it is true, without the full measure of success, others almost to perfection. It was, I believe, not the want of a type, but of the genius to give expression to the type, or again it was the power of convention, that prevented those artists whose works have survived from enabling us to settle from their productions the question which has engaged us. The type of horse portrayed on the frieze was a very old one, even in the fifth century; the minute description of the points given by Xenophon and confirmed by other writers, helps us to detect the faults which a Greek horseman would have seen in some of the figures on the frieze. To obtain, therefore, a correct conception of the Greek idea of a good horse, one should compare the first chapter of Xenophon's treatise with the best animals on the Parthenon. Some assistance may be had from the brief summary of the defects of a horse as given by Pollux* (1,191). These are as follows: —

"Horn thin, hoofs full, fat, soft, flat, or, as Xenophon calls them, low-lying. Heavy fetlocks, varicose veins in the shanks, flabby thighs, hollow shoulder-blades, projecting neck, mane bald, narrow chest, head fat and heavy, large ears, nostrils converging, sunken eyes, thin meagre sides, sharp backbone, rough haunches, thin buttocks, stiff legs, knees hard to bend."

There is one point, however, which seems to call for special notice, and that is the mane. As I have already said, Schlieben has fallen into the common error of believing that the writers require the mane to be long, but that in works of art it is nearly always cut short. But a careful reading of the authors will show that the word "long" is never applied to the mane by any of them. The adjectives are "thick," "full," "fine-

* See note 76.

haired," "crinkly," and it is said to fold over to the right All these expressions might be applied to a short, and the first even to a hogged, mane. Xenophon comes nearest to calling the mane long when he uses the phrase ἕως ἂν κομῶσιν, which I have rendered "while it is flowing" (chap. v, p. 32). But the context shows that it is there a question of mane or no mane, not of short or long. And there is nothing in the chapter to show that Xenophon disapproved of keeping the mane down by trimming; there must be plenty to take hold of in mounting, he says, and enough for beauty. On the other hand, it is evident that he would have had no hogging of the mane, and none of the other writers mention such a thing. But Xenophon's very insistence on the beauty of a flowing mane seems to me to show that not all the world agreed with him; he is as earnest about it as if he were a member of the Humane Society preaching against docking. It is not surprising to me, therefore, to find in works of art the portrayal of a different fashion. Probably most people, if asked to describe the mane of the Greek horse, would say that it was hogged; at least, that is the answer which I have almost invariably received on putting the question. There can be, I think, no doubt that the hogged mane was a fashion which existed in Greek antiquity, silent about it though the writers may be; the difficulty is to discover whether it always existed side by side with the flowing mane, or whether it went out of fashion after a certain period. Still harder would it be to determine whether hogging was practised only upon horses of a certain breed or size, as it generally is with us, or upon horses intended only for special purposes. Into these questions I have not entered, but I believe light might be cast upon them by a careful study and comparison of works of art.[77] A mere glance through such a well-known book as Baumeister's "Denkmäler des Klassischen Altertums" shows a number of examples of hogged manes. Omitting for the moment the Parthenon marbles, striking instances will be found as follows: the Oropus relief, p. 69; Phigalia frieze, plate xliv; very ancient terra cotta from Melos, p. 1290; Dipylon vase, p. 1943; Mycene vase, p. 1941; black-figured vase, p. 2081. But it would be a great mistake to suppose that the hogged mane is the only fashion in art. In the same book examples of long straight or long curly manes are found as follows: black-figured vases, pp. 67, 725; Corinthian vase, p. 1962;* altar of Pergamon, p. 1257; Vienna cameo, p. 1390; François vase, plate lxxiv; Trajan's column, p. 2057. Short and curly manes are to be seen; for instance, on a late vase, p. 728, and a Pompeian wall-painting, p. 667. It is a dangerous thing to offer an opinion on such a point without much more exhaustive research than I have made; but I have been led to believe, from these and many pictures in other books, that the hogged mane was an old fashion, which in the time of Xenophon was passing away.[78] Although I admit that much is to be said on the other side, yet I am strengthened in this belief by observing that out of nearly a hundred horses on the Parthenon friezes only about thirty have hogged manes, and that frequently these thirty have an unfinished look in other points, so that many of them, as works of

* I give an illustration of this vase on page 22.

THE GREEK RIDING-HORSE. 95

art, are of inferior quality. It should be said, however, that the manes of the pediment horses are all hogged.

In size, it is clear that the ancient Greek horse was smaller and not so tall as ours. His descendants in their own country still retain this characteristic feature. We might infer from the whole tone of the descriptions by the writers, that they were speaking of a small and compactly built animal, although we find no exact statements of size or height. But there is one passage at the beginning of Xenophon's seventh chapter which is very significant. It appears that an approved method in mounting was to " lay hold of the mane *about the ears*." We should need no further evidence than this to prove that Athenian cavalry horses were much less high than the ordinary saddle-horse is now; but it is supported by the illustrations in art, and especially by the reliefs of cavalry horses on the Parthenon. But just here let me say that I believe that most people fancy the Greek horse a great deal smaller than he really was. This is because they judge him from the Parthenon frieze and other compositions, such as vase-paintings, in which he appears side by side with men standing on the ground. The unthinking observer, comparing the height of the horses with the height of the men in the same composition, and finding that the men are usually as tall or even taller than the horses, concludes that the Greek horse must have been a very small animal indeed. But such a conclusion is made in ignorance or in neglect of an important principle of Greek art. By this it was required that in a composition of numerous figures the heads of all should be nearly upon a level, whether the men were walking, riding, or driving. This principle, called *Isokelismos*, does not in practice offend the eye, which, recognizing the effect of the whole as a work of art, is not troubled by the exactness of levels, untruthful to nature though it may be. But of course it utterly forbids us to use the apparent height of the men in such a composition as any standard for the real height of animals. A better means of judging from the frieze is by observing how far the feet of the riders hang down below the bellies of their horses. The distance appears to be much greater than in the case of men on horseback to-day. It should be remembered, however, that the cella frieze was placed more than thirty-five feet above the floor of the temple, and that the outer row of columns prevented the spectator from standing at a distance to examine the frieze. He had to look almost straight up. In the British Museum, as well as in others, the slabs or casts of them are placed much lower. But in their original position, the perspective would prevent the feet of the men from seeming to dangle so far below the bellies of their horses.* The difference, however, would be slight, and the whole build of the horse in these as well as in other works of art, stamps him as a small animal. Of course the size and height of horses varied then just as now. The differ-

---

* Since I wrote the above, my friend Dr. Hayley informs me that he heard Professor Kekulé make the same remark in a course of lectures on the frieze Professor Kekulé also observed that the sculptors of this frieze had anticipated some of the discoveries made by instantaneous photography in the positions of the horse in motion.

ent breeds may have had their distinctions in this respect; but, as I have said, we know nothing of them. It may be significant, however, that on Thessalian and Macedonian coins the riding-horses often appear equal in size to our own. Little, if anything, can be inferred from the almost giraffe-like proportions of the animal on the most archaic vases.

From the physique of the horse I pass to his nature. In reading Xenophon's treatise one may be struck by the frequency with which this man, well used to riding as he was, refers to the horse as a dangerous animal to come near. While it should be remembered that the Greeks generally used entire horses, not geldings, for all purposes and especially for war, yet this will not wholly account for Xenophon's constant tone of caution; and it is probable that the process of domestication, extending through centuries, has made a very great difference in the temperament of the animal, as we know it, from what it was in the classical period. Ancient literature is not without its stories [79] of the devotion of the horse to his master; but even in these the wildness or the savageness of the animal is generally brought out, showing itself often in a bloody revenge taken by the steed upon the warrior who has killed his rider, or in absolute refusal on the part of the horse to be mounted by any save his accustomed rider. There is, in fact, nothing to show that the Greek ever made a friend of his horse, least of all that there was ever between them that beautiful relation which is so common between horse and man in Arabian tales. Even the poets, from Homer down, did not appreciate what might be made of it. Witness the answer of Achilles to his horse Xanthus when the noble animal did his best to warn his master: "Xanthus, why prophesiest thou my death? Nowise behooveth it thee;" and he puts him off with scarcely less harshness than that of Balaam to his ass.[80] Xenophon probably comes as near to loving the horse as any Greek ever did, and no modern humanitarian was ever more earnest in urging over and over again the principle of treating horses with kindness. His precept, "Never deal with the horse when you are in a passion," is a whole treatise in itself. But he has not a single word of love for the horse anywhere, and does not even suggest that the rider should try to win his horse's affection for its own sake. All his teaching is practical: be kind to your horse and he will do as you desire. The explanation of all this may be that to the Greeks the horse suggested war, with all the merciless qualities which characterized it in antiquity. They kept no riding-horses in our sense of the word, and we never read of a Greek as taking a ride for pleasure. Their horses were bred and reared primarily to be machines of battle, or for the scarcely less fiercely contested struggles in the hippodrome. They had but a slight place in the every-day life of men; to be sure, they were sometimes used on journeys, especially over mountains; but even ambassadors generally travelled on foot, and carriages were usually drawn by mules. The pomps and processions on festive days were so contrived as to be part of the horse's training for war. His real business lay among warriors; for he was like the horse in Job that "saith among the trumpets, Ha, ha; and he smelleth the battle afar off, the thunder of the captains and the shouting." *

It may be appropriate, then, to finish this sketch by setting down what is known of the famous charger of Alexander the Great. The names and characteristics of many horses of gods or heroes have been transmitted to us; but Bucephalas is the only horse belonging to a mortal about which the Greeks have left any particular description.[81] He was of the best Thessalian breed, black, with a white star, and very large. As Gellius says, "Et capite et nomine Bucephalas fuit." The fact is that, long before this famous animal, a well-known type of Thessalian horses had given rise to the name, which means "Bull-head."[82] This type had small ears set well apart, thus leaving the brow wide and the poll large. "Some people," says an unknown writer in the "Geoponics," "reckon among the finest horses those with eyes which are not a match; such, they say,

---

* Cf. Vergil, Georgics, III, 83:—

Tum siqua sonum procul arma dedere,
Stare loco nescit, micat auribus et tremit artus,
Collectumque premens volvit sub naribus ignem.

was Bucephalas." If this story is true, he had what is sometimes called a "China eye." King Philip bought him from one Philoneicus, a Thessalian, — for thirteen talents, as Plutarch says; for sixteen, according to Pliny (from thirteen to eighteen thousand dollars). Either price is probably an absurd exaggeration, the result of the later reputation of the animal. Evidently the king was not a believer in Xenophon's principle of giving a horse a thorough trial before buying him; for, says Plutarch, when they brought the king's new purchase into the place where they were to try him, it appeared that he was a fierce and unmanageable beast. "He would neither allow anybody to mount him, nor obey any of Philip's attendants, but reared and plunged against them all, so that the king in a rage bade them take him away for an utterly wild and unbroken brute. But Alexander, who was by, cried out, 'What a fine horse that is which they are spoiling! The clumsy cowards, they can't handle him.' Philip said nothing to this at first; but when his son kept on grumbling, and seemed to be in a great taking, he said at last, 'Are you finding fault with your elders because you know any more yourself, or can handle a horse any better than they?' 'I could handle that horse, at any rate, a great deal better than anybody else,' was the answer. 'And what will you forfeit for your rashness if you fail?' 'The price of the horse, by Zeus!' There was a burst of laughter, and it was so agreed. In a moment Alexander ran up to the horse, seized the reins, and turned him to face the sun; for it seems that he had observed that what frightened the creature was the sight of his own shadow playing to and fro on the ground before him. After a little patting and coaxing, seeing him full of courage and spirit, Alexander quietly slipped off his cloak, and springing up bestrode him unharmed. Feeling the bit gently with the reins, he restrained him, without whipping or hurting him, until he saw that the horse had given up all threatening behavior, and was only hot for the course; then he let him go, and urged him on by raising his voice and using his heel. The attendants of Philip were anxious and silent at first; but when he turned and came back full of just pride and pleasure, they all raised a cheer, except his father. But he, they say, wept for joy; and after Alexander had dismounted, said, 'You must go look for a kingdom to match you, my son; Macedonia is not large enough for you.'"

Alexander was only a boy of twelve when this happened; for it was before Aristotle became his tutor, — an event which took place when the prince was thirteen. Bucephalas, however, was no young colt, but fourteen years old even then. Ever after, though he would allow the groom to ride him bareback, yet when his trappings were on he suffered none save Alexander to mount him; others who tried it met with the same savage behavior which he had shown at his first trial, and were forced to take to their own heels to save themselves from his. But he bent his knees when Alexander appeared, so as to make mounting easy, without waiting for the word of command. For the rest of his life he was Alexander's favorite charger, and went with the great king on his expedition to the East. In Hyrcania he was stolen, but was returned in a hurry on proclamation that unless he was brought back the whole nation — men, women, and children — should be cut off. "Thus," remarks Arrian, "he was as dear to Alexander as Alexander was terrible to the barbarians." He carried the king in all his great victóries, and finally died at the age of thirty* from wounds received in the battle against the Indian king Porus in 327 B. C. Alexander, says Gellius, had pressed recklessly forward into the very ranks of the enemy, and was the mark for every spear. More than one was buried in the neck and flanks of the horse; but though at the point of death, and almost drained of blood, he turned, carried the king with a bold dash from the very midst of the foe, and then and there fell down, breathing his last tranquilly now that his master was safe, and as comforted by it as if he had had the feelings of a human being. No wonder that Alexander founded the city of Bucephalia in his honor, and grieved for him as if he had lost a friend; no wonder that of this horse only in all Greek

* The usual extreme limit, according to Aristotle, of a horse's years. See page 127.

literature is it written that he was dear to his master.

It is generally believed that the fine bronze found at Herculaneum* is a reduced copy of the figures of Alexander and Bucephalas from the famous group which was made by Lysippus, at Alexander's own order, to represent a scene at the battle of Granicus. Of another likeness of Bucephalas we have only a well-known anecdote. Alexander once went to see his own portrait with that of his horse, painted by Apelles. The king did not praise the picture as it deserved. But his horse, on being brought up, neighed at the horse in the picture as if it were a real animal; whereupon, "Your Majesty," said Apelles, "your horse seems to be a good deal better judge of painting than you are."

* See cut on page 69.

POINTS OF THE HORSE.

THE following are the descriptions of a good horse, according to the ten Greek and Roman writers referred to on page 86.

SIMON.

On Simon and his work, see page 119. I have translated from the text of Blass, "Liber Miscellaneus editus a Societate Philologica Bonnensi," 1863,

p. 49 ff. The fragment here translated is all that remains of Simon's book on the horse, except a few quotations from it in Pollux.

IF one desires to know this subject well, it seems to me that the shape of the horse is the first thing. To begin with the country of birth, you must know that, so far as Greece is concerned, Thessaly is the best. As to size there are three accepted terms, — large, small, and good-sized, or, if you like, moderate; and it is obvious which size each of the terms will fit. But moderate size is best in every animal. I cannot tell a good horse from his colour; however, it seems to me that a mane which is of the same colour throughout and of fine hair is generally the best, and besides it is most unlike that of the ass and the mule. A point second to none in consideration is that the horse must be short above and long below, so that the distance shall be short from the withers to the haunches, but as long as possible from the hind legs to the fore; next, that he must be sound-footed. A good hoof for a horse is the light and handy sort, neither broad nor too high, and having little flesh but

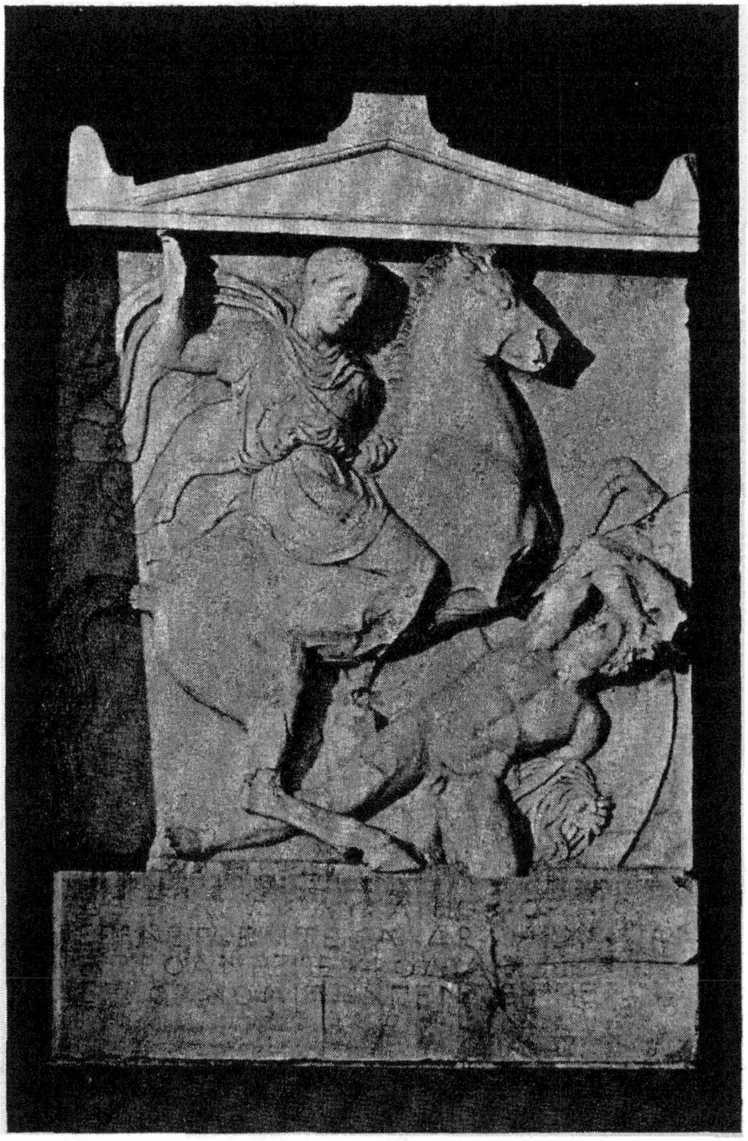

thick horn. The sound is also a sign of the good hoof; for the hollow sort has more of the cymbal ring than the full and fleshy. Let him have supple pasterns and no stiffness of the fetlock joints; his shanks should be shaggy, with the parts about the back sinew and the shank sinewy and with as little flesh as possible up to the knee. Above, however, the leg should be fleshier and stouter. Let the space between the two legs be as wide as possible, for then he can throw out his legs without interfering. His chest should be neither too narrow nor too broad, and his shoulder-blade very large and very broad indeed. Let the neck be slender near the jaw, supple, flattened back to the rear, but bending down to the front from the slenderest part. The head should be advanced, and the neck not short. Let him have a high poll, and a head flat-nosed but light; the nostrils should be very large, the jaws slender and a match for each other, the eyes large, very prominent and bright, the ears and teeth small, the jaw as small as possible, and the part between the neck and the jaw very slender. The withers and seat should be very large, the sides very broad and deep, and the loin supple (you can tell that the loin is supple if he does not stand on both his hind legs at the same time, but is constantly changing from one to the other), the haunch very large and broad, the flank very small. The gaskins should not be very fleshy; and he should have small stones. Between the hams he should not be prominent nor full, but only rather swelling a little, and the breech should be very small and well out of sight. Let him hold his tail high, and have it thick at the base and long. This for the shape of the horse. He is by far the best that has all these points; and second is he that has the majority of them, including those which are of the most service. The colt begins to be driven two years after birth. About this time he sheds his first teeth, when he is thirty months old; the second a year after, the last in another year or in less time; and he is at his prime for swiftness and courage at six years old.

VARRO.

This extract is taken from the "Res Rusticae," 2, 7, 5. The book was written in 37 B.C., when the author was eighty years of age. The translation is made from the Latin text of Keil.

WHAT the horse is to be like can be guessed from the colt, if it has a small head with well-marked parts, black eyes, nostrils not narrow, ears close to the head; mane thick, dark, rather crinkly, and of fine hair, folding over to the right side of the neck; broad, full chest; large withers, moderate-sized belly, flanks drawn in as you go down, broad shoulder-blades, tail full and crinkly; shanks stout, matching, shaped off somewhat towards the inside; knees round and not large, hoofs hard. The veins should be visible all over the body, convenient for treatment when he is not well.

VERGIL.

From the "Georgics," 3, 79 ff., published about 29 B.C. Translated from the text of Ribbeck.

LOFTY is his neck and brisk-moving his head; short in the barrel is he, plump of back, his undaunted breast swelling with folds of muscle. The bays and grays are noble beasts; the poorest colour is white and yellow. Then, when arms clash afar, he cannot keep the spot, but pricks up his ears, quivers in every limb, and clouds roll from his fiery nostrils. His thick mane on his right shoulder falls, and there it lies; his chine is double where it runs along the back, and his firm-horned hoof rings loudly as he paws the ground to hollows.

CALPURNIUS SICULUS.

From the "Eclogues," 6, 52 ff., written probably between 57 and 60 A.D. Translated from the Latin by E. J. L. Scott.

> MY beast displays
> A deep-set back; a head and neck
> That tossing proudly feel no check
> From over-bulk; feet fashioned slight,
> Thin flanks, and brow of massive height;
> While in its narrow horny sheath
> A well-turned hoof is bound beneath.

COLUMELLA.

From "De Re Rustica," 6, 29, 2 ff., written a little before 65 A.D. Translated from the Greek text of Schneider.

SMALL head, black eyes, nostrils flaring, short ears set up straight; neck supple and broad without being long; mane thick and hanging down on the right side; broad chest with the muscles bulging out everywhere; large straight shoulders; sides curving, seat double, belly drawn in, stones small and alike, broad flanks sinking in; tail long, thick, and crinkly; shanks supple, deep, and straight; knee well-turned, small, and not turned in; rounded buttocks; thighs bulging with muscles everywhere; hoofs hard, high, hollow, and round, topping off with moderate-sized coronets.

OPPIAN.

From the "Cynegetica," 1, 176 ff., a poem written in the first part of the third century. Translated from the Greek text of Schneider.

LET him be large himself and round of limb, but small be the head he raises high and loftily above his neck; lofty his crest, but let the jaw come down low, inclining towards the throat; broad and beautiful should be his front between the brows, and from above let thickly clustering locks fall about his face; under the brow his bright eyes flash with ruddy fiery light; wide are his nostrils, small his ears, and fair-sized his mouth; his neck well rounded, shaggy with the mane, like the helmet with its nodding flowing crest; wide his chest, the barrel long, back broad, chine double, and loins plump; his long-haired tail should flow out far behind him; his thighs should be well-knit and muscular; below, his shank bones should be straight and long, round, handsome, free from flesh, like the long-antlered stag's whose feet are storm-swift; his pasterns sloping, his round hoofs coming well up above the ground, compact, horny, and strong.

NEMESIAN.

From the "Cynegetica," verse 245 ff., written in the second half of the third century. Translated from the Latin text of Haupt.

HIS back is smooth and broad of surface; flank very long; the belly small, even on large animals; brow lofty, ears mobile, head handsome, and crest high; eyes flashing with radiant light; his neck mighty and arching back to his stout shoulders; the breath of his hot nostrils rolls forth like steam; his foot loves not the task of standing still, but his hoof smites the ground continually, and his high spirit wearies out his own limbs.

APSYRTUS.

Apsyrtus was a veterinary surgeon under Constantine the Great in the first part of the fourth century. The translation is from the compilation called the "Geoponics," 16, 1, 9 ff.

SMALL head, black eyes, nostrils not converging, ears erect, neck supple; mane thick, somewhat crinkly, and falling on the right side of the neck; chest broad and muscular, shoulders large, forearms straight, belly well-rounded, stones small; seat preferably double, otherwise not humped; tail large and crinkly-haired, shanks straight, thighs muscular; hoof of a good contour, and equally solid on all sides; frog small, horn hard

PELAGONIUS.

Pelagonius lived in the last half of the fourth century. The translation is from the new edition of his "Ars Veterinaria," § 2, by M. Ihm, Leipzig, 1892.

SMALL head, black eyes, nostrils open, ears short and pricked up; neck flexible and broad without being long; mane thick and falling on the right side; broad and muscular chest, big straight shoulders, muscles sticking out all over the body, sides sloping in, double back, small belly, stones small and alike, flanks broad and drawn in; tail long and not bristly, for this is ugly; legs straight; knee round, small, and not turned in; buttocks and thighs full and muscular; hoofs black, high, and hollow, topping off with moderate-sized coronets. He should in general be so formed as to be large, high, well set up, of an active look, and round-barrelled in the proportion proper to his length.

PALLADIUS.

From the "De Re Rustica," 4, 13, 2 ff., written probably about the middle of the fourth century. Translated from the Latin text of Schneider.

IN a stallion four things are to be tested, — his shape, colour, action, and beauty. For shape we shall try for a large compact body, height to suit his strength, a very long flank, big round haunches, breast broad, the surface of the body all closely knotted with muscles; foot dry and firm, the horn which forms its shoe hollow and pretty high. The points of beauty are a small dry head, with scarcely anything but mere skin on its bones; ears short and mobile, large eyes, wide nostrils, neck erect, mane thick, tail even fuller, hoofs set on firm and round. In action, let him be high-spirited, swift-footed, quivering-limbed (a proof of courage), and willing to be put to speed from a dead halt and to stop in the midst of a fast dash without making trouble. The principal colours are chestnut, golden, albino, bay, brown, fawn, yellowish, checkered, dead white, piebald, glistening white, black, dark. Of less value and of various degrees of beauty, black mixed with albino or chestnut, gray with any other colour you like; dappled, spotted, mouse-colour, or even duskier. But in the case of stallions, let us pick out a single distinct colour; others are to be disdained unless great merit in other ways makes up for defect in colour. The same points must be considered in brood mares; especially they should have long large barrels and bodies.

NOTES.

1. (PAGE 13.) Simon was an Athenian, but we do not know exactly when he lived and wrote. The story of his criticism of Micon's picture (see p. 85) sets the earliest limit (Micon was a contemporary of Polygnotus, who was in Athens about 460 B.C.), and Xenophon's mention of him the latest. Various theories have been propounded, such as W. Helbig's, who thought (A. Z. 1861, p. 180) that he was the Simon mentioned in Aristophanes (Knights, 242), and that he was Hipparch in 424 B.C.; and Gerhard's, who recognized him in the figure of a charioteer inscribed with his name on a vase (Auserlesene Vasenbilder, iv, taf. 249). But the earliest known Greek prose which has survived is the tract on the Athenian State, written between 424 and 413 B.C.; and the fragment of Simon's work (see p. 107) bears no evidence of being older, and is probably not so old. It is likely that it was written at the beginning of the fourth century. Xenophon, in speaking of Simon, scarcely uses the tone which would have been proper in speaking of a very ancient writer. Besides the long fragment a few short ones are preserved in Pollux. According to Pliny (Nat. Hist. 34, 76), a statue of Simon dressed as a knight was made by Demetrius (who flourished probably in the latter half of the fifth century); but this may be only a mistaken allusion to the statue of the horse mentioned by Xenophon. It is supposed by Ernst Curtius (Die Stadtgeschichte von Athen, p. 188), who calls Simon a contemporary of Pericles, that this statue was intended to embody a perfect representation of the ideal horse, just as the famous work by Polycleitus illustrated the proportions of the ideal man; but this is of course a mere theory, unsupported by literary evidence.

2. (PAGE 13.) The Eleusinion, in Athens, was a precinct of Demeter, Kore, and Triptolemus, with two temples; it often served as the goal of processions, especially cavalry displays.

3. (PAGE 14.) This excellent advice stamps Xenophon at once as a true horseman. Horace, though he was no rider, knew the doctrine too; witness Sat. 1, 2, 86 : —

"Regibus hic mos est, ubi equos mercantur: opertos
Inspiciunt, ne si facies, ut saepe, decora
Molli fulta pede est, emptorem inducat hiantem
Quod pulchrae clunes, breve quod caput, ardua cervix.
Hoc illi recte;"

which may be rendered, —

Swells, when they buy horses, have a way of covering them up when they look them over, for fear that a handsome shape set upon tender feet, as often happens, may take in the buyer as he hangs open-mouthed over fine haunches, small head, and stately neck. And they're right in it.

4. (PAGE 14.) Throughout this book it should be remembered that the ancients did not shoe their horses. The Romans, indeed, used for mules the *solea*, a sort of sock of leather completely covering the hoof and tied about the fetlock, strengthened underneath by a plate of iron (Catullus, 17, 26). Nero substituted plates of silver (Suetonius, Nero, 30), and his luxurious wife, Poppaea, gold (Pliny, Nat. Hist. 33, 140). But we do not hear of socks for horses, except that in the retreat of the Ten Thousand an Armenian showed the Greeks how to wrap their horses' feet in little bags when travelling through deep snow. But of course all this is quite different from the modern practice of permanent shoeing. This latter is first mentioned in literature in the time of the Emperor Justinian, the first half of the sixth century (Martin, Les Cavaliers Athéniens,

p. 400); but shoes were probably known earlier. It is said that one was found in the tomb of King Childeric, who died in 460 A.D. There is a cut of it, taken from Montfaucon, in Ginzrot, ii, tab. 86, 1. The cut makes it practically identical with the modern shoe; but Beckmann, in his " History of Inventions," justly doubts the trustworthiness of the picture.

5. (PAGE 15.) The Greek word used by Xenophon is χελιδών, which literally means "swallow;" and the frog was so named from its resemblance to the forked tail of the bird. In later Greek we find it called βάτραχος, "frog" (Geoponics, 16, 1, 9, from Apsyrtus), and in Latin *ranula*, "little frog" (Vegetius, 1, 56, 31). The French call it *fourchette*; the Germans *Strahl*. It will be observed that Xenophon's principle (supported by the other writers) of keeping the frog well up from the ground, and calling for a high and hollow hoof is not always accepted in modern times.

6. (PAGE 15.) This remark, and many of the works of art show that it was not the custom to trim down the fetlocks. In warm climates they do not grow very long, and instead of disfiguring the foot serve rather to set off its contour.

7. (PAGE 16.) The Greek word is περόνη, which has given much trouble to translators and commentators. It means literally the pin of a brooch,

— the Greek brooch being shaped somewhat like the modern safety-pin. In the anatomical writers it was naturally applied to the small bone in the man's arm or leg, — the radius or fibula. In the horse, of course, this bone is above what we call his "knee;" and Xenophon, who has not yet reached this knee, cannot be thinking of a part above it. Hence it has generally been believed that he meant a bone in the knee itself, one of the astragals. But I believe that Xenophon was not thinking of the skeleton, but rather of the animal as he looked in the flesh. Indeed he may not have understood the anatomy of the horse in its relation to man's; certainly below he speaks of the forearm as if it corresponded to the upper instead of to the lower arm in man. What, then, was more natural than that he should compare the back sinew to the small bone of man's leg? This granted, he has described what naturally follows when a horse with "gummy" legs (just what he has been speaking of) is put to hard work. He breaks down, or gives way in the back sinews. This explanation seems to have occurred to none of the commentators, — not even to Dindorf, though he had the advantage of using the fragment of Simon (see p. 109) in which the word περόνη is used exactly as in Xenophon. I am happy to be supported in my view of the passage by Dr. Lyman, Dean of the Harvard Veterinary

School, to whom I submitted my opinion. After reaching it, I found that the same translation of the word was used by Stonehenge (see p. 89).

8. (PAGE 16) I have used the word "forearms" for greater clearness. Xenophon calls them thighs (μηροί), applying the same word to the fore as later to the hind legs. No special horse dialect had yet developed; but the same words, so far as possible, were used of horses as of men.

9. (PAGE 16.) The lean, dry head with small bones, was esteemed the most beautiful; and this point is insisted upon by all the ancient writers except Nemesian, who says merely that the head should be handsome.

10. (PAGE 17.) Xenophon seems to mean the "bars" here. Their fineness was a thing not to be seen by the eye, but to be discovered by trial in riding, as he says in the third chapter, in his remark about the Volte.

11. (PAGE 17.) The reason for this requirement, so well recognized for race-horses, is well stated by Professor Flower in his admirable little book called "The Horse: a Study in Natural History" (p. 142, American edition): "Owing to the great length of the soft palate and its relation to the upper end of the windpipe, breathing takes place entirely through the nose. When men, dogs, and many other animals, in consequence of any great exertion, begin to pant and require an additional quantity of air to that which is ordinarily taken in by the nose, the mouth comes to the aid of that channel and is widely opened; but the horse under the same circumstances can only expand the margins of the nostrils, for which action there is a very efficient set of muscles, acting on the cartilaginous framework which supports them and determines their peculiar outline."

12. (PAGE 17.) Small ears, set well apart so as to leave a large poll, formed the type of beauty which gave rise to the name Bucephalus (βουκέφαλος, "bull-" or "ox-headed"). This was applied to a valuable breed of Thessalian horses (Aristophanes, Frag. 135) long before it was given, in a slightly modified form, to Bucephalas, the famous charger of Alexander. Examples of this type are the bronze head in the Uffizi and the famous marble head by Phidias (see frontispiece and plate facing p. 83).

13. (PAGE 17.) The idea is that in well-built horses, in good condition, the flesh rises on each side of the spine so that the latter does not stick up like a ridge but lies in a slight depression. This quality was of course even more highly appreciated before the days of saddles than it is now. It is mentioned also by Vergil, Columella, Oppian, and Apsyrtus.

14. (PAGE 18.) The word used here, ὑπόβασις, is very vague, and has given rise to various interpretations. I think it refers to the act of gathering in the hind legs in doing the demi-pesade, described in the eleventh chapter.

15. (PAGE 18.) This fact is noted also by Aristotle (Part. Anim. 4, 10, 12) and Pliny (Nat. Hist. 11, 260), who state that young quadrupeds can reach their heads to scratch them with the hind feet; Pliny adds that they cannot graze without bending the forelegs. Buffon independently observed these facts. Schlieben (p. 86) gives two Arabian methods of estimating what will be the height of horses. By the first a cord is stretched from the nostril over the ears and down along the neck; this distance is compared with that from the withers to the foot; the colt will grow as much taller as the first distance exceeds the second. By the other method, the distance between the knee and the withers is compared with that from the knee to the coronet; if it has reached the proportion of two to one, the horse will grow no taller.

16. (PAGE 20.) See p. 75.

17. (PAGE 23.) By the word "markers," γνώμονες, Xenophon means the milk-teeth, and he is therefore advising against the purchase of a horse over five years old. The times of the shedding of

NOTES.   127

these teeth were well understood by the ancients, as we know from Aristotle, Hist. Anim. 6, 22, 12; Varro, Res Rusticae, 2, 7, 2; Apsyrtus in the "Geoponics," 16, 1, 12. What we now call the "marks" are of course in the permanent teeth; they are spoken of by Varro, Ibid. 2, 7, 2; Columella, 6, 29, 4; Apsyrtus, Ibid. 16, 1, 12. Aristotle sets the average age of horses at from eighteen to twenty years; some, he says, live to be twenty-five or thirty; and with great care a horse may live to be fifty, though thirty is generally the highest limit (Hist. Anim. 6, 22, 8).

18. (PAGE 24.) The word here and in chapter seven is πέδη, which properly means "fetter." Godfrey Hermann, in his essay on the words which the Greeks used to denote the gaits of the horse (Comment. Lips. p. 59), has shown that the Volte is meant in these passages.

19. (PAGE 24.) He seems to mean that if, for example, the stable lies to the right, the horse will throw his head to the left, and advancing his right shoulder, will make a bolt for it. The left rein being loose and the right side of the mouth hard, the rider will have no control over the animal. But the passage is obscurely worded, and has been variously interpreted. It may mean "unless they are hard-mouthed and also are directed towards home."

20. (PAGE 27.) The stable was part of the townhouse, and was situated on one side of the front door. In the country it may have been an outbuilding.

21. (PAGE 27.) Aristotle (Oeconomica, 1, 6, 4) tells of a Persian who was asked, "What is the best thing to make a horse plump?" and who answered, "His master's eye."

22. (PAGE 28.) Barley was the ordinary feed for Greek horses. Apsyrtus says that the disease was an indigestion coming from eating when out of breath after a journey or a run. Among the symptoms he mentions that the horse is doubled up, cannot bend his legs, and refuses to move, throws himself down, and takes his food lying. A like account is given by Vegetius (Mulomedicina, 5, 43, 1). Aristotle calls the disease incurable "unless it cures itself" (H. A. 8, 24, 4).

Besides barley, Greek horses were frequently fed on spelt, sometimes on hay; and wheat is mentioned two or three times by Homer. A mash of barley and green herbs was prescribed in cases when a mash would now be given.

23. (PAGE 28.) Courier tried the experiment, and describes it as follows: "À Bari, ville maritime de la Pouille pierreuse, on garnit le sol d'une écurie construite pour quatre chevaux, d'un lit de cailloux pris sur la plage, et arrondis par la mer, dont les plus gros pouvaient avoir le volume d'un boulet de quatre. Ce lit, de dix-huit pouces à peu près de hauteur sous la mangeoire, qui fut exhaussée d'autant, s'abaissait en pente vers le mur opposé. Trois chevaux y furent placés pieds nus : l'un, poulain de quatre ans, race des environs de Cirignola, qui n'avait jamais eu de fers ; l'autre, de huit ans, d'Acquaviva, ferré ordinairement de devant ; le troisième, vieux cheval de troupe. De ces trois chevaux, le premier seulement avait le sabot bien fait et la corne assez bonne. On les pansait à l'écurie, d'où ils ne sortaient que pour la promenade ; on mettait sous eux la nuit, au lieu de litière, quelques brins de sarment. Leur urine tombant à travers les pierres sur le pavé très-uni de l'écurie, s'écoulait à l'ordinaire avec l'eau qu'on y jetait de temps en temps pour nettoyer la place ; de sorte que le cheval était toujours à sec. Chaque jour, soir et matin, le poulain trottait plusieurs reprises à la longe, sur la grève, où l'on avait amassé des cailloux pareils à ceux de l'écurie. Au bout de deux mois et demi, sa corne était plus compacte, et la fourchette surtout avait acquis une solidité remarquable. Il fit le voyage de Bari à Tarente passant par Monopoli, Ostuni, Brindisi, Lecce, Manduria, tous chemins de traverse remplis de pierres, et revint sans être ferré ni incommodé : à la vérité on ne l'avait monté que deux jours ; mais il aurait résisté à de plus grandes fatigues, et il était aisé de voir que les mêmes soins continués l'auraient mis en état de se passer de fers toute sa vie ; il fut vendu. Les deux autres n'eurent pas le même succès : leur corne, gâtee par les clous, se fendait et s'exfoliait pour peu qu'ils marchassent ; mais peutêtre qu'avec le temps ils se seraient fait un bon pied.

"Cette épreuve eut lieu dans les mois juillet, août et septembre ; on ne peut douter qu'elle n'eut complètement réussi sur des chevaux calabrais, qui ont meilleur pied que ceux de la Pouille."

Stalls paved as Xenophon describes are not by any means unknown both here and in England. The late E. F. Bowditch, Esq., of Framingham, was a strong believer in them, though he would by no means have approved the hollow hoof described in Xenophon's first chapter. But of course his horses were shod, and so shod that the frog and heel were very close to the ground. His object in using the cobble-stones was to stimulate the growth of those parts, and to keep them soft so as to prevent the frog from shrivelling. This softness of the frog and its contact with the ground, he thought, prevented all jar on the foot, the frog acting as a buffer.

24. (PAGE 29.) The Greek cared for his body by bathing and rubbing as well as by the free use of oil. Hence Pollux (1, 201) advises rubbing the horse's bars with the fingers to make them fine, and washing the mouth and lips with warm water and anointing them with oil.

25. (PAGE 31.) The muzzle was of thin bronze, perforated like a sieve, or of bronze wire or wicker. See cut, p. 34.

26. (PAGE 31.) It was the custom among the Greeks and Romans to give the horse a roll in fine sand after he had exercised. So Pheidippides in the "Clouds" of Aristophanes (32), after a dream of horse-racing, calls out in his sleep to his slave to give the horse a roll and take him home. And Isomachus in Xenophon's "Oeconomicus" (11, 18) has his slave do the same thing after his morning's ride. This Isomachus was a fine type of the Athenian of the best period,— pure-minded, honourable, and upright. He was a lover of the country and a fearless rider; and the following account which he gives Socrates of the way in which he was wont to spend his mornings makes a delightful picture. The translation here given was made by Gentien Hervet in 1532. I copy from the edition of 1537 (Thomas Berthelet, printer, London).

"I ryse in the mornynge out of my bed so yerly, that if I wold speke with any mā, I shall be sure to fynde him yet within. And if I haue any thynge ado in the citie, I go about it, & take it for a walke. And if I haue no matter of great importance to do within the citye, my page bryngeth my horse afore in to the fieldes, and so I take the way to my groũd for a walke, better parauenture, than if I dyd walke in the galeries and walking places of the citie. And whan I come to my grounde, and if my tenantes be eyther settynge of trees, or tyllyng or renewyng the grounde, or sowynge, or caryenge of the fruite, I beholde howe euerye thynge is done, and caste in my mynde, how I might do it better. And afterwarde for the moste parte, I gette me a horsebacke and ride as nere as I can, as though I were in warre constrayned to do the same, wherefore I do not spare nother croked wayes, nor noo shroude goinges up, no ditches, waters, hedges, nor trenches, takynge hede for al that, as nere as can be possible, that in this doing, I do not maime my horse. And whã I haue thus doone, the page leadethe the horse trottynge home agayne, and caryeth home with him into the citie, out of the cõtre that that we haue nede of. And so than I get me home againe, somtimes walkyng, and sometime runnynge. Than I wasshe my handes, and so go to dyner good Soc. the which is ordeyned betwene bothe, soo that I abyde all the daye nother voyde nor yet to ful."

Besides the charm of its language, this translation is very accurate; there is in it but one real error, for Xenophon does not say that the page leads the horse "trotting" home, but that he "gives him a roll" and then leads him home.

27. (PAGE 31.) Pollux (1, 185) mentions several. The σπάθη, which he describes as wooden and shaped like a feather, was used for cleaning the hair. The word really means "any broad blade;" and this implement is doubtless to be recognized on an Assyrian relief from Nimroud, representing the stable of Assurnazirpal. Other implements were the ψήκτρα, for combing out, of iron with teeth like a saw, corresponding to our curry-comb; and the σωρακίς, which seems to have been a sort of mitten of purple cloth, used by the groom in rubbing down and to give a gloss to the coat.

28. (PAGE 32.) This prescription goes back to Homer, Il. 23, 280, "a charioteer . . . who on their manes full often poured smooth oil, when he had washed them with water." The Scholiast on these lines says: "This is why Xenophon recommends the washing of the head and forelock with water;" and he adds the irrelevant but interesting information that about a sixth of a pint of oil was enough to supple a man's whole body.

29. (PAGE 32.) Upon this passage Berenger (The History and Art of Horsemanship, by

Richard Berenger, Gentleman of the Horse to His Majesty: London, 1771) has the following interesting note (Vol. I, p. 239) :—

"These observations are so true and just that one could almost think it needless to dwell upon them; yet such is the cruelty and absurdity of our notions and customs in 'cropping,' as it is called, the ears of our horses, 'docking' and 'nicking' their tails, that we every day fly in the face of reason, nature, and humanity. Nor are the present race of men in this island alone to be charged with this folly, almost unbecoming the ignorance and cruelty of savages; but their *forefathers*, several centuries ago, were charged and reprehended by a public canon for this absurd and barbarous practice; however, we need but look into the streets and roads to be convinced that their descendants have not degenerated from them; although his present Majesty, in his wisdom and humanity, has endeavoured to reclaim them, by issuing an order that the horses which serve in his troops should remain as nature designed them:

'Who never made her work for man to mend.'—DRYDEN."

"The title of the canon is,—

"19. *Ut reliquias rituum paganorum quisque abjiciat.*

Equos vestros turpi consuetudine detruncatis, nares finditis, aures copulatis, verum etiam et surdas redditis, caudas amputatis; et quin illos illaesos habere potestis, hoc nolentes cunctis odibiles redditis. Equos etiam plerique in vobis comedunt, quod nullus Christianorum in Orientalibus facit; quod etiam evitate.

"From the influence of a vile and unbecoming custom, you deform and mutilate your horses, you slit their nostrils, tie their ears together, and by so doing make them deaf; besides this you cut off their tails; and when you enjoy them uninjured and perfect, you chose rather to maim and blemish them, so as to make them odious and disgustful objects to all who see them. Numbers of you likewise are accustomed to eat your horses,—a practice of which no Christians in the East were ever guilty. This also you are hereby admonished to renounce entirely."

This canon was number nineteen among those passed at the Council of Calcuith, held in 787 or 785 A. D. It may be found in Spelman's Councils of England, I, p. 293.

30. (PAGE 32.) Aristotle, Aelian, Plutarch, and Pliny all repeat this strange story. Sophocles evidently knew it; I translate from a fragment (598) of his "Tyro":—

> For my lost locks I mourn, like some young mare
> That rustic drivers catch and hale away
> To where their rude hands in the stables reap
> The golden harvest clean from off her neck
> They drag her to the mead; in its clear streams
> Mirrored the semblance of her form she sees,
> Her mane with that foul cropping shorn away.
> Oh, then e'en pitiless might pity her,
> Cowering with shame and like to some mad thing,
> Mourning and weeping for the mane that's gone.

On the mane in general, see p. 91 ff.

31. (Page 35.) Xenophon says "left;" the Greeks had no technical terms like our "near" and "off."

32. (Page 36.) The strap which goes over the crest back of the ears.

33. (Page 36.) The word used by Xenophon means properly "net." It is applied to the whole upper part of the bridle with its different straps. The cheek-straps, the headpiece, with the straps running from this, beside the ears, to the front, and often joining a strap which ran down the middle of the face, all formed a sort of network.

34. (Page 36.) When a leading-rein or halter was attached to the bridle (see note 38), this caution would not be necessary; for such a rein was fastened to the nose-band or chin-strap, and hence, if it had any pull at all on the jaws, it pulled on both alike. Xenophon means that in the absence of such a halter *both* the bridle-reins must be grasped at once.

35. (Page 37.) By this method the helper took the foot or knee of the rider in his hand, and so raised him. It is recommended for the elder men in the cavalry by Xenophon in his treatise on the "General of Horse," 1, 17. It was the privilege of Tiribazus, Satrap of Armenia, when he was at court, to mount the King of Persia in this fashion

(Xen. Anab. 4, 4, 4). A special attendant for this purpose is said to have accompanied Alexander in his battles (Arrian, Anab. 1, 15, 8). At the court of Philip, pages, sons of noblemen, performed this duty for the king (Ibid. 4, 13, 1). Slaves, however, seem to have "made a back;" and the Roman Emperor Valerian, when prisoner to Sapor, was obliged by that haughty prince to mount him in this degrading fashion, and not to offer his hand (Lactantius, " De mortibus persecutorum," 5).

36. (PAGE 37.) By a very neat touch, Xenophon fancies himself on the horse's back, speaking to him encouragingly.

37. (PAGE 38.) Stirrups were unknown till long after the Christian era began. Other methods of mounting are described in the next chapter; but here we see that horses were sometimes taught to stoop or settle down so as to make it easier for the rider to reach his place. This was done in two ways: (1) by bending the knees, and thus lowering the shoulders; (2) by throwing the fore feet forward and the hind feet back, thus lowering the seat, as horses sometimes do naturally when tired. The second is the method here spoken of by Xenophon, who applies to it the word ὑποβιβάζεσθαι. Pollux (1, 213) describes it by saying that in it the horse set his legs apart,

settled in, and lowered himself. A rider about to mount by this method is represented on the frieze of the Parthenon, and on a vase from Nola (see cut on p. 39). That it was employed sometimes by Roman soldiers is evident from a relief in Clarac, Musée des Sculptures, Plate 221. But it is not referred to elsewhere in Greek literature. Courier had seen this method in use in Germany, and Jacobs says that it was introduced thither from England (!) and called *Strecken*. Alexander's horse Bucephalas was taught the first method, — that of bending the knees (Curtius, 6, 5, 18). This method is represented on a black-figured vase in the Hermitage collection (see cut on p. 30). The Greek word in this case is ὀκλάζειν.

38. (PAGE 39.) From this it appears that a strap or cord, entirely distinct from the reins, was attached to the bridle, doubtless to be used in leading as well as in mounting. (See note 34.) It may be seen in the cuts on pp. 34, 39, and 29, in which it is attached to the chin-strap. On a vase-painting in Gerhard (Auserlesene Vasenbilder, iv, 293, 294, 1) it is attached to the nose-band. A leading-rein just like the Greek is to be seen in Assyrian reliefs.

39. (PAGE 39.) As Greek bits had no branches, the chin-strap was not the equivalent of our curb-chain, and no leverage came from pulling on it.

It merely kept the bit in place and the mouthpiece from slipping through, and would cause no pain if pulled down by the halter. The nose-band was of leather or metal. On the bits, see note 53.

40. (PAGE 39.) The Roman soldier referred to in note 37 has his hand here. This remark of Xenophon's throws light on the height of the Greek cavalry horse. (See p. 95.) Mounting-blocks were often used. There are several on the frieze of the Parthenon, and one on the Gjölbaschi Heroon (Taf. 23, B. 2). They were placed at convenient intervals along the streets in Rome by Gaius Gracchus (Plutarch, 7, 2).

41. (PAGE 39.) In this method of mounting, the spear must have been used much as we use a vaulting-pole (but of course with only one hand). It is absurd to suppose that there was a little projection or crossbar towards the butt of the spear, which served as a step in mounting. The athletic Greek would have scorned such a thing. A gem in the Stosch collection, supposed to represent a warrior mounting in that fashion, is capable of a different interpretation; and the spears in Stuart and Revett (Antiquities of Athens, iii, p. 47) have nothing on them but the common thong to help in hurling. Yet the crossbar theory has found credence with Ginzrot, Berenger, Winckelmann, Jacobs, Schlieben, and Martin, as well as with all the commentators on Xenophon's work except Courier, who will have none of it. He describes the way in which the Polish and Austrian lancers of his day, as well as the Cossacks, were in the habit of mounting; and doubtless this is very like what Xenophon meant: " Ils saisissent de la main gauche les rênes et une poignée de crins, et s'appuyant de la droite sur la pique, un peu penchée vers la croupe du cheval, ils s'enlèvent tout d'un temps, en mettant la pied à l'étrier, et le cavalier se trouve en selle la lance en main."

42. (PAGE 41.) The Greeks had no saddles with trees, nor the Romans until the fourth century, so far as can be judged from works of art. They rode either bareback or upon a cloth which was fastened by a girth under the belly or about the breast of the horse. In works of art the girths are often omitted.

43. (PAGE 42.) This statement seems to be exactly the reverse of the truth; for the horse in starting to canter turns himself slightly across his line of progress, in order to enable him to lead with that leg which is advanced by this turn. Hence to lead with the left, he turns his head to the right and his croup to the left. Accordingly there has been much discussion of this passage in Xenophon, and various emendations of the text have been proposed by modern editors. Hermann, after various attempts, practically gives the passage up; and so far no satisfactory explanation or emendation has been offered. I have endeavoured to translate the Greek exactly as I found it. If the Greek text is as Xenophon wrote it, I cheerfully admit that any absurdity in the translation is due to my own misunderstanding of the Greek rather than to any ignorance on the part of Xenophon. It should also be observed that the lead recommended (with the left) is not the favourite lead to-day.

The walk, trot, and gallop are the only gaits mentioned in Greek authors. The amble or pace was certainly unknown to them until after the time of Aristotle, who says ($\pi\epsilon\rho\grave{\iota}$ $\zeta\acute{\omega}\omega\nu$ $\pi o\rho\epsilon\acute{\iota}\alpha s$, 14) that if a horse moves the two legs on the same side at the same time, he must fall. Still it will be observed that on the Orvieto vase (see cut facing p. 76) the horses are all moving in this manner. But as Körte shows (A. Z. 1880, p. 181), this had become the conventionalized manner of representing the motion of the horse. It is found in Assyrian and Egyptian art, and from thence passed to the Phoenician and the archaic Greek, where it is the regular rule, although some exceptions are found. It appears on coins down to the best period, and on red-figured vases of the more severe type. It was, therefore, not intended to represent a natural gait in the animal. Pliny (N. H. 8, 166) mentions a Spanish breed of horses whose natural gait was the amble, and adds that this led to the belief that the trot was in all breeds an acquired gait.

44. (PAGE 46.) The Greek spur had no rowels, but was merely a small goad fastened to the heel by straps which passed over the instep and under the sole. Such spurs have been found in Olympia and in Magna Graecia, and are represented in vase-paintings. A book on the development of the spur, with many beautiful plates, is " Der Sporn in seiner Formen-entwicklung," Zchille und Forrer, Berlin, 1891.

45. (PAGE 47.) The Odrysians were a Thracian tribe, whose power, once extending from the Strymon to Abdera, declined at the end of the fifth century B. C.

46. (PAGE 47.) This seems at first sight a device entirely unworthy of a horseman, and Berenger strongly condemns it; but it is evident, from what follows, that Xenophon's intention was not to recommend one to support himself by the mane, but to prevent the beginner (this book was written for "the younger of his friends") from disturbing the horse in his leap by jerking at the bit. The context shows that it was with the bridle-hand (thus kept motionless) that the mane was to be grasped. The expression "it is not a bad thing" is probably purposely selected; and Xenophon does not here say, as usual in this book, "it is well." Of course a practised rider would need no such help as the mane to keep his hand quiet. On the frieze of the Parthenon the rider who has his right hand on his horse's head is merely soothing the excited animal (see cut facing p. 89).

47. (PAGE 48.) As Jacobs observes, the rule is a good one, but the reason given for it (and repeated by Pollux, 1, 206) seems to be exactly the reverse of the truth. The horse, as a rule, prefers familiar places, and after constant riding over one road it will be found very difficult to make him go elsewhere.

48. (PAGE 48.) For instance, on Xenophon's estate in Scillus they hunted deer, wild boars, and gazelles; among other animals, hares, bears, and wolves are frequently mentioned as hunted in Greece. The hunt was one of the principal amusements of both Greeks and Romans, as it had been of earlier nations. Much information on the subject will be found in Xenophon's "Cynegeticus," though the work treats chiefly of dogs and hounds, and in the treatise of the same name by Arrian.

49. (PAGE 52.) The words in brackets are, as Cobet pointed out, a stupid interpolation, adding nothing to what has been said already.

50. (PAGE 53.) On the bits see note 53.

51. (PAGE 54.) "Chirrup" is here used, for want of a better word, to translate ποππυσμός, a noise made by the lips alone. It is used of a kiss (Anthologia Palatina, v, 245 and 285), and therefore does not mean "whistling," as it is generally translated here. The sound is familiar to every rider, but we use it now to start a horse. By "clucking," κλωγμός, is meant the sound made by the tongue against the roof of the mouth.

52. (PAGE 54.) This advice looks as though Xenophon were hurried, or as if a lazy horse were too distasteful a subject for him to treat. He could not have meant it to be followed to the letter.

53. (PAGE 56.) There is no evidence for a curb-chain on a Greek bit, and hence Greek bits had no leverage. The reins in every case acted directly on the mouthpiece of the bit. Nor do we hear of two bits used at the same time, nor of two sets of reins. In this passage Xenophon recommends two kinds of bits, — the smooth and the rough; but it is evident from his language that these were not the only kinds used in his day. Here, however, I am concerned only with these two. What constituted the smoothness of the one and the roughness of the other? Certainly not

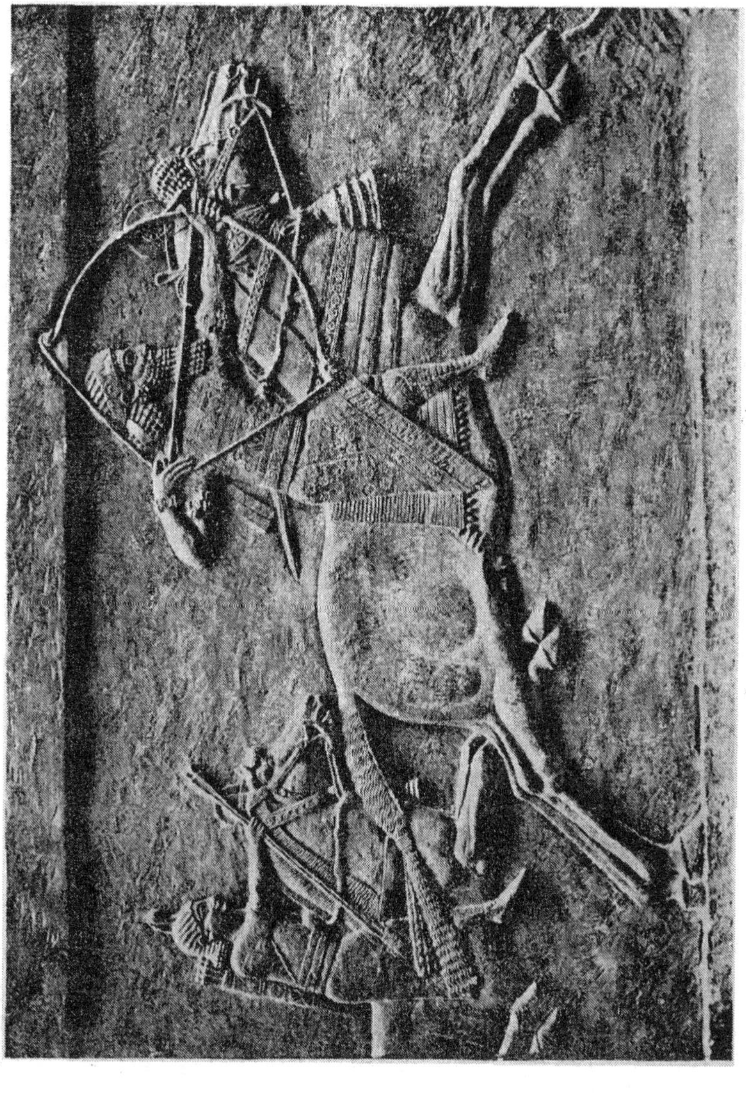

the discs (τροχοί); for they were used on both kinds, and were actually smaller on the rough than on the smooth. Evidently, therefore, the difference lay in the nature of the "echini;" this word, the plural of "echinus," I have felt it necessary to transfer from the Greek bodily, for we have none in English which will exactly express its meaning here. The word in Greek, ἐχῖνος, means "sea-urchin;" therefore the contrivance upon the mouthpiece of the bit was probably round, and had on its edges prickly spines, such as we see on the edges of the sea-urchin's shell. In the rough bit these spines were sharp; Xenophon's language suggests that there were echini on the smooth bit, but that their spines in this case were not sharp. Fortunately, light is thrown on this subject by a bit which has actually come down to us from antiquity. This bit (see cut, p. 50) was found on the Acropolis of Athens in 1888, when the wall and other works of Cimon were in course of excavation. It lay among the débris used as filling at the time of these works. The bit is therefore very old, dating back nearly, if not quite, to the time of the Persian wars, 490–479 B.C. I take the picture, with part of my description, from an article by Lechat in the "Bulletin de Correspondance Hellénique," 1890, p. 385. The mouthpiece is jointed, and the reins were attached to the large rings at each end. What appear to be branches are not like the branches of our curb-bits; for they did not serve to support a curb-chain, nor was a rein attached to them. They were fastened to the cheek-pieces of the bridle, and merely kept the mouth-piece in place. Each cheek-piece divided into two straps, just before reaching the bit, to which they were attached at the two small holes in each branch. This arrangement for attaching the bit was a very old one; it may be seen on many Assyrian reliefs (see cut facing p. 145) and on some Greek vases (see cuts on pp. 20, 23, 27, 39).* See also the Dodona statuette, p. 44. These pictures show that the branches lay close against the sides of the mouth; in the picture of the Acropolis bit (and in that of the Carapanos bit below) the perspective is misleading. It is evident that no leverage was to be had from such branches. We cannot tell whether the bit which Xenophon had in mind was attached in this way or not; he himself says nothing, and such branches are altogether wanting

* On this subject, see an article in the "Revue Archéologique," 1888, p 52, where it is shown that a prehistoric bit found in Switzerland and one found in the Caucasus region were attached in the same way as above described. The latter almost exactly resembles the Acropolis bit; the former has no echini, but is a mere twisted snaffle. In treating the bit, I do not think it safe to use the illustrations given in Montfaucon or in Jacobs.

in many works of art. But to return to the echini. Each part of the mouthpiece of the Acropolis bit has little spines on it; but these spines are rounded and not sharp. Further, to judge from Lechat's description, they rise directly from the mouthpiece itself, and not from a cylinder put on about the mouthpiece. But we know that the echini were not always actually part of the mouthpiece; we might infer that they were not, from Xenophon's remark about "all the parts put on round the joints;" and this inference is made certain by the construction of another ancient bit (cut on p. 60). This bit, also described by Lechat, is in the Carapanos collection of bronzes; but unfortunately its country of origin and its age are unknown. Like the other, it is jointed; but each half of the mouthpiece forms an axis about which play an echinus and a large disc, the latter being biconvex like a lens. The spines of the echini are very sharp. The discs are evidently what Xenophon calls the τροχοί. But in this bit we have a combination which he does not recommend; that is, we have "good-sized" discs, whereas he says that with sharp echini the discs should be heavy, but not so high as they are when used on the smooth bits. It is inconceivable, however, that the discs should ever have been higher than these. This bit was attached to the cheek-pieces by the small rings on

148 XENOPHON ON HORSEMANSHIP.

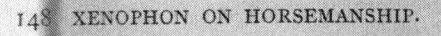

the ranches; the reins were fastened to the large
hoo which play about the axes of the mouth-
piec. The branches are very large; I know of
only one parallel for them in art, on a vase published in the "Journal of Hellenic Stud
plat 2, fig. 6, and possibly on the coi
on 26.

w, it is clear that neither of th
spo s exactly to Xenophon's de
fro them I have, I b
wh he meant than
commentators on h
fro Xenophon,
bit hence the di
like the rollers
Th sharp ec
hor if he at
had been ta
subituted.
so at they
rea inflic
get ng so
it, rge dis
jaw apart
beteen th
an these
is prese
Grek w
 nop

NOTES. 49

a single piece of metal (though the Greeks may
have had such bits), but always speaks of one that
is jointed. His expression, "stiff bit," therefore,
applies to one in which the parts — the joints,
discs, and echini — do not play easily about
each other, either from rust, or because the parts
too tight.

 at nu   kinds of bits, and vari-
   upon   ds, were known to
 nts, i   e classical writers, fr
  , an   art. For example, t
              the mouth of Alexa-
              if one may trust t
              nzi di Ercolano,"
              he Naples Museu
              have seen pho
              resemble the
              several approa
              ct is a good fi
              le confidence c
              nd in the ordina

              ce of hanging litt
              e bit is familiar

              stance, in the Pan
              of the Partheno
              occasion. A co

the branches; the reins were fastened to the large hooks which play about the axes of the mouthpiece. The branches are very large; I know of only one parallel for them in art, on a vase published in the "Journal of Hellenic Studies," 1890, plate 2, fig. 6, and possibly on the coin in the cut on p. 26.

Now, it is clear that neither of these bits corresponds exactly to Xenophon's description. But from them I have, I believe, got a clearer idea of what he meant than is to be had from any of the commentators on his book. The horse, we gather from Xenophon, was to be trained on the rough bit; hence the discs were low and heavy, probably like the rollers used on some modern curb-bits. The sharp echini acted on the "bars" of the horse if he attempted to seize the bit. When he had been taught his lesson, the smooth bit was substituted. Here the echini were rounded, so that they merely suggested punishment without really inflicting it. But to prevent him from getting so used to the smooth bit as not to mind it, large discs were put on, "to make him keep his jaws apart and drop the bit." These discs were between the bars and the tongue, on each side; and, these once understood, we see why the horse is represented with his mouth open in nearly all Greek works of art.

Xenophon does not recognize a bit consisting of

a single piece of metal (though the Greeks may have had such bits), but always speaks of one that is jointed. His expression, "stiff bit," therefore, applies to one in which the parts — the joints, discs, and echini — do not play easily about each other, either from rust, or because the parts are too tight.

That numerous other kinds of bits, and variations upon these two kinds, were known to the ancients, is evident from the classical writers, from Pollux, and from works of art. For example, the modern roller-bit is found in the mouth of Alexander's horse (cut on p. 69), if one may trust the large engraving in the "Bronzi di Ercolano," ii, p. 339. There are also in the Naples Museum a number of bits, of which I have seen photographs. None of them exactly resemble the bit described by Xenophon, though several approach it in details. The whole subject is a good field for closer investigation, and little confidence can be placed in the statements found in the ordinary books on antiquities.

54. (PAGE 58.) The device of hanging little rings from the middle of the bit is familiar in modern times.

55. (PAGE 61.) As, for instance, in the Panathenaic festival. The frieze of the Parthenon represents the parade on this occasion. A comment by Beulé will be found interesting here (L'Acropole d'Athènes, 2, p. 160): "La troupe s'avance au galop, par un mouvement plein d'ensemble, mais d'une allure retenue et qui n'a rien d'impétueux. Les chevaux semblent galoper sur place, ou plutôt se cabrer gracieusement. Si l'on veut une description du cheval du Parthénon, qu'on lise le onzième chapitre du traité d'equitation. Le type idéal que cherche Xénophon, Phidias l'a constamment copié. La race thessalienne offre encore aujourd'hui une certaine ressemblance avec les bas-reliefs de la frise."

56. (PAGE 62.) That is, of course, when the forelegs are raised in the movement described in the next sentence, the "demi-pesade." By "loin" here he means the hollow on each side below the ribs, — the flanks.

57. (PAGE 63.) Xenophon refers to the phylarch and hipparch, respectively. See p. 75.

58. (PAGE 64.) See cut on p. 61.

59. (PAGE 65.) The cuirass ordinarily consisted of two metal plates made to fit the body, one protecting the breast and abdomen, and the other the back. They were hinged on one side, and buckled on the other. They were further kept in place by leathern straps or bands of metal, passing over the shoulders from behind and fastened in front and by the belt. About the lower part of the cuirass was a series of flaps of leather or felt, covered with metal, but flexible, protecting the hips and groin without interfering with freedom of movement (see cuts on pp. 19 and 69). There were also similar flaps at the right shoulder to protect the part of the body which was left exposed when the arm was raised to hurl the javelin or to strike with the sword. But even in the time of Xenophon, a sort of scale armour was not unknown, the metallic scales being fastened to a cuirass of felt. On the frieze of the Parthenon one of the riders wears a combination of plate and scale armour, the breast and back being covered by plates which are joined at the sides by scale armour. Of course all parts of the cuirass were often elaborately ornamented. Xenophon's insistence on the point that the cuirass should be made to fit the individual reminds one of the conversation reported by him in the "Memorabilia" (3, 10, 9 ff.) between Socrates and a cuirass-maker.

60. (PAGE 65.) The neck-piece is rarely seen in art, but is found on certain reliefs from Pergamon (Altertümer von Pergamon, ii, 43, 44, 2, and 47, 2). It comes up between the shoulder-straps, and is at the back of the neck, not at the front. So in the statuette of the Etruscan warrior, called the Mars of Todi; see Baumeister, taf. lxxxix.

But a cuirass with the neck-piece extending all the way round has been found at Grenoble (Baumeister, p. 2044), and is represented on the coin which serves as the tail-piece to Chapter I (p. 19). It is probable that this piece was an Eastern device, suggested to Xenophon during his campaign in Persia, and not generally adopted in Greece.

61. (PAGE 66.) It is impossible to say what Xenophon meant by a Boeotian helmet. There were two principal types of Greek helmets, — the Corinthian and the Attic, to be seen on the head of Athene on the coins of Corinth and Athens respectively. The Corinthian, having a nose-piece and immovable cheek-pieces, was the more complete protection. The Athenian generally had cheek-pieces, always movable, however, so that they could be turned up, leaving the face free. These do not always appear on the coins. Both helmets protected the nape of the neck. But as Xenophon has provided for the protection of the throat by a special piece rising from the cuirass, he can scarcely mean the Corinthian helmet which covers this part pretty effectually; and his description would conform even less closely to the Attic type.

62. (PAGE 66.) Examples (but not of Greek origin) of this flexible piece of armour have been

found at Olympia and at Pergamon (Curtius and Adler, Olympia, tafelband iv; Altertümer von Pergamon, ii, taf. 43). It was made of strips of metal, lapping over each other like the fingers of a mediaeval gauntlet. See also Baumeister, Denkmäler, p. 2028.

63. (PAGE 66.) Greaves were made of elastic metal, lined with felt or leather, and were snapped about the leg below the knee and then fastened behind with straps or buckles. Such a piece is here recommended to fit the right arm; and on the analogy of the leg-greave I suppose that it was intended for the part of the arm below the elbow.

64. (PAGE 67.) That is, the part near the shoulder and the armpit; this is left unprotected by the unfolding of the flaps mentioned above.

65. (PAGE 67.) The armour here prescribed for the horse is not Greek, but Oriental. We find no evidence of its use in Greece in the art or literature of the fifth century. Xenophon, doubtless, became acquainted with it during the Expedition of the Ten Thousand, approved it and desired its introduction into Greece. It was introduced to a limited extent in the fourth century. But there is nothing in art to explain how the thigh-armour of the horse protected the rider's legs.

66. (PAGE 67.) Here the Greek word is $\ἔποχον$; but just before and in chapter seven (see note 42) the usual word for the cloth, ἐφίππιον, is used. It is not certain what the difference was between the two; but probably, as Schlieben thinks, the ἔποχον was more extensive; and was padded or quilted (see the great Pompeian mosaic of the battle of Issus); perhaps it was continued under the belly.

67. (PAGE 67.) Such boots may be seen on the frieze of the Parthenon and on the Orvieto vase (cut facing p. 76).

68. (PAGE 67.) The words "sword," "sabre," and "scimitar" are used only as approximations here. The Greek swords of all sorts were much shorter than ours; and the two latter forms resembled curved butcher's-knives rather than swords, in our sense of the word.

69. (PAGE 68.) See the Orvieto vase (cut facing p. 76).

70. (PAGE 68.) The "Hipparchicus," or "Cavalry General;" see p. 71.

71. (PAGE 74.) There are only three passages, and two of them (Iliad, 15, 679; Odyssey, 5, 371) are in similes; hence they may and doubtless do refer, not to the heroic period in which the scene of the poem was 'laid, but to the later time when the verses were written. The third is the only passage in which heroes are actually described as riding on horseback (Iliad, 10, 513); but this is in the Dolopeia, universally admitted to be the latest part of the Iliad in order of composition. It cannot, therefore, be accepted as evidence in the face of the general practice of driving, found everywhere else in heroic scenes.

As my book is concerned only with the later practice of riding, there is no need to discuss the very obscure question of the introduction of the horse into Greece, shadowed forth as it may or may not have been by the myths of Pegasus, the Centaurs, Erechtheus, and Poseidon. According to Pietrément (whom I quote at second-hand, having never seen his book, as I remarked in my preface), no fossil remains of horses have been found in Greece; and the animal was certainly introduced thither, though the route is unknown.

72. (PAGE 76.) The price of the horse branded with the letter Koppa, in Aristophanes' "Clouds," 20. The exact significance of this and other brands is unknown, save that horses thus branded were of more than ordinary value. See cut on p. 184, and its description.

73. (PAGE 84.) See Pliny, N. H. 35, 95; Aelian, V. H. 2, 3.

74. (PAGE 85.) Pseudo-Lucian, Dem. Encom., 24; Aelian, V. H. 14, 15.

75. (PAGE 85.) Aelian, H. A. 4, 50; Pollux, 2, 69.

76. (PAGE 87.) The description by Vegetius (fifth century) in the "Mulomedicina," 4, 6 (6, 6) is of a particular breed, and that not a Greek one. Isidorus, Origines, 12, 1, 45 (seventh century), and Pollux, 1, 188 ff. (second century) are mere compilers, adding nothing in this matter to the knowledge which we have from other sources.

77. (PAGE 93.) Light may come from another direction. We find now and then that the manes of horses were shorn as a sign of mourning. This was done by Persians on the death of Mardonius (Hdt. 9, 24), and by Greeks on the deaths of Pelopidas and Hephaestion (Plutarch, Pelopidas, 33; Alexander, 72). In the Alcestis of Euripides, 428 ff., the bereaved husband orders all his subjects to shear the manes of their horses.

78. (PAGE 94.) Not a Homeric fashion, however, (see *e.g.* Iliad, 17, 439). It was intermediate between the Heroic and the Classical Age.

79. (PAGE 98.) See Pliny, N. H. 8, 156 f.

80. (PAGE 99.) The horse Xanthus and his mate wept for the death of Patroclus; but their grief was not appreciated by the charioteer Automedon (Iliad, 17, 426 ff.).

NOTES. 157

81. (PAGE 101.) Our information comes from Plutarch, Life of Alexander, 6; 32; 61; Morals, p. 970 D; Arrian, Anabasis, 5, 14, 4; 19, 4 ff.; Strabo, p. 698; Gellius, 5, 2; Geoponics, 16, 2; Curtius, 6, 5, 18; 9, 3, 23; Pliny, N. H. 8, 154; Aelian, V. H. 2, 3.

82. (PAGE 101.) See Aristophanes, frag. 41, Kock.

ON THE ILLUSTRATIONS.

IN making selections from the antique for the pictures in this book, I have been guided, not so much by the interest or beauty of the originals, considered as works of art, as by their usefulness in explaining or illustrating the various subjects which have been treated in the foregoing pages. So, too, the following brief notes are not written from the point of view of the art-critic, an office to which I do not pretend; but in them I have given the immediate source from which each illustration is taken, the museum or collection in which the object itself is to be seen to-day, and, wherever possible, the time of its production, and the place where it was found. I have mentioned, also, the points in each work which led me to choose it for the purposes of this book. Without too great presumption I may venture to remark that but few, if any, of the Classics, except Homer, have been thus closely and fully illustrated from ancient art. The present attempt may serve to show what an opportunity there is in this direction.

FULL-PAGE ILLUSTRATIONS.

FRONTISPIECE. Bronze head in the Uffizi, Florence, No. 426 of the bronzes in the collection in that gallery. From a photograph. The work was found near Città Vecchia, and was sent from Rome to Florence in 1585, according to the catalogue of the Uffizi gallery. The time of its production is unknown. Originally there was a bridle on the head; the mouthpiece of the bit still remains. This head has the ears wide apart, leaving the poll large (see p. 17); and it therefore illustrates the type of beauty which gave rise to the term βουκέφαλος (see note 12, p. 125).

PAGE 17. From the frieze of the Parthenon, a work completed about 440 B. C. under the direction of Phidias (see pp. 84 and 97). From a photograph in "Masterpieces of Antique Art," by S. Thompson. Although this slab is not in as perfect a state of preservation as are some of the others, yet it has always been among the most

ON THE ILLUSTRATIONS.   161

admired for the grace, action, and truth to nature of its figures. The horses seem to illustrate exactly the type preferred by Xenophon in his first chapter (see also p. 89). For the costume of the riders see the remarks on p. 163.

PAGE 41. Fragment of a sixth-century monument in honour of an Athenian warrior of a time much earlier than the Persian wars. From "Die Attischen Grabreliefs," Conze, i, taf. 9. The original is in the Barracco collection in Rome; Conze took his engraving from a cast in Strasburg. The complete work was a tall, narrow stele, like the well-known stele of Aristion. On the upper part was represented the dead man, armed probably as a hoplite; only his feet and the butt of his spear remain. Below, in what is called the κρηπίς of the monument, is a young horseman, holding the reins in his left hand and in his right two javelins; he is armed also with a short, straight sword. It should be remembered that the two reins are often represented on the same side in early art, so that this relief does not prove the existence of two sets of reins (see note 53, p. 144). The reins must be supposed to be attached directly to the bit; there is here no representation of branches, but such details are often neglected in art. This rider, however, carries two javelins; and yet Xenophon in his twelfth chapter (p. 68) speaks as if he were recommending something entirely new in suggesting the use of two javelins instead of one spear. But the technique of this work shows that the rider is of a time long before Xenophon; further, on a number of early vase-paintings (see for instance pp. 30 and 65), two javelins are carried by cavaliers. I am not aware that any explanation has been offered of this apparent contradiction. When it is remembered, however, that the Athenians had no regularly organized body of cavalry before the Persian wars (see p. 75), it may be thought that after the organization of the force it was armed merely with one spear; and that in the transition state before this organization, hoplites, when mounted for some special purpose, carried two. Thus, the present monument may have represented the dead warrior serving in two capacities, — on foot and as a mounted hoplite. It is true that the rider in the Lamptrae relief (facing p. 68) carries but one spear; and so the custom probably varied before the knights were organized.

PAGE 68. Part of a fragment of a monument found in the Attic deme of Lamptrae, and now in Athens. From the "Mittheilungen des deutschen arch. Instituts in Athen," xii, taf. 2. A work of perhaps a little after the middle of the sixth century. See the remarks just above, and note that the regular Athenian cavalry did not carry shields. The rider wears the usual short mantle. The horse is a much better animal than the one represented in the plate just treated; on his gait see p. 141. Another horse is led at the left as the outlines show. This is not uncommon in art.

PAGE 76. From an Attic cylix, or cup, found at Orvieto, in Central Italy, described and illustrated by G. Körte in the "Archäologische Zeitung," 1880, taf. 15. It is now in the Berlin Museum. The picture represents the examination for admission to the Athenian cavalry, the δοκιμασία (see p. 76). At the left, just below the handle of the cup, is a bearded man seated under a tree, with a stylus and a writing-tablet in his hands. In front of him stands a man with a long staff (the cup is here broken). Towards them are approaching three young men, dressed alike, not in armour, but in the usual gala or parade costume of the cavalry, — a chlamys, or short cloak, buckled at the shoulder; a petasus, or broad-brimmed hat; and κόθορνοι, or high riding-boots (actually, the artist has represented these boots only in the case of the second rider). Each brings up his horse by a leading-rein (see note 38, p. 138), not by the bridle (see note 34, p. 136); the bridles in fact are here left to the imagination, and the leading-rein is supposed to be attached to the chin-strap or nose-band. In the cut on p. 39 the bridle-rein and the leading-rein are distinguished, the thick dark streak representing the latter. The horses, Körte thinks, are not represented in a natural gait (see p. 141); yet perhaps not much evidence on this point can be got from a representation of horses moving at a walk (see p. 163). Each man carries two javelins (see p. 162). The horses have long tails, long forelocks (see p. 32), and hogged manes (see p. 93). Behind the first horse stands a young man (also under a tree), with a peculiar staff having a crook at the upper end. This man may be the hipparch or the phylarch (see p. 75) of the troop undergoing examination, for we know that young men were chosen to these offices. Finally, behind the third horse stands a bearded man with a staff of office. The two upright bearded men are doubtless the examining committee of the Senate; the seated man is their secretary. The first knight is actually in course of examination, as his upright and attentive position shows; the second is on his way, the third just starting. The newly discovered treatise of Aristotle on the Athenian Constitution gives us some interesting and in part new information about this examination (chap. 49). In the centre of the bottom of the cup is one of the two hundred mounted bowmen, called the Scythians, employed by the Athenians as a sort of police force.

ON THE ILLUSTRATIONS.

PAGE 83. Head of one of the horses of Selene, the moon goddess, from the eastern pediment of the Parthenon, now in the British Museum. From a photograph in Brunn's " Denkmäler Griechischer und Römischer Skulptur," lief. 38. On the eyes, see p. 83; on the mane, p. 95; and on the Bucephalus type of the head, p. 125.

PAGE 89. From the frieze of the Parthenon, as engraved in "Ancient Marbles in the British Museum," viii, pl. 18, and edited by Hawkins. This group affords a most perfect idea of the type of horse approved by Xenophon (see p. 89). I have remarked, at the end of note 46 (p. 143), upon the soothing gesture of the second rider; every foot of his horse is raised from the ground. The third rider is one of the few on the frieze that wear the cuirass (note 59, p. 150); he has also a helmet of the Attic type with folding cheek-pieces (note 61, p. 152), and wears boots (p. 67). But the fifth rider and horse are the best of all; I quote Hawkins here: "Nothing can exceed the vigour, the life, the animation which pervades the whole horse, bounding from the earth with the very exuberance of animal spirits; the muscular power and elasticity with which he springs from the ground is admirably expressed, as are also the playful pawings of the forelegs and the animated expression of lively impatience in the muscles and positions of the head and neck. Nor and the leading-rein are distinguished, the thick dark streak representing the latter. The horses, Körte thinks, are not represented in a natural gait (see p. 141); yet perhaps not much evidence on this point can be got from a representation of horses moving at a walk (see p. 163). Each man carries two javelins (see p. 162). The horses have long tails, long forelocks (see p. 32), and hogged manes (see p. 93). Behind the first horse stands a young man (also under a tree), with a peculiar staff having a crook at the upper end. This man may be the hipparch or the phylarch (see p. 75) of the troop undergoing examination, for we know that young men were chosen to these offices. Finally, behind the third horse stands a bearded man with a staff of office. The two upright bearded men are doubtless the examining committee of the Senate; the seated man is their secretary. The first knight is actually in course of examination, as his upright and attentive position shows; the second is on his way, the third just starting. The newly discovered treatise of Aristotle on the Athenian Constitution gives us some interesting and in part new information about this examination (chap. 49). In the centre of the bottom of the cup is one of the two hundred mounted bowmen, called the Scythians, employed by the Athenians as a sort of police force.

ON THE ILLUSTRATIONS.

PAGE 83. Head of one of the horses of Selene, the moon goddess, from the eastern pediment of the Parthenon, now in the British Museum. From a photograph in Brunn's " Denkmäler Griechischer und Römischer Skulptur," lief. 38. On the eyes, see p. 83; on the mane, p. 95; and on the Bucephalus type of the head, p. 125.

PAGE 89. From the frieze of the Parthenon, as engraved in " Ancient Marbles in the British Museum," viii, pl. 18, and edited by Hawkins. This group affords a most perfect idea of the type of horse approved by Xenophon (see p. 89). I have remarked, at the end of note 46 (p. 143), upon the soothing gesture of the second rider; every foot of his horse is raised from the ground. The third rider is one of the few on the frieze that wear the cuirass (note 59, p. 150); he has also a helmet of the Attic type with folding cheek-pieces (note 61, p. 152), and wears boots (p. 67). But the fifth rider and horse are the best of all; I quote Hawkins here: " Nothing can exceed the vigour, the life, the animation which pervades the whole horse, bounding from the earth with the very exuberance of animal spirits; the muscular power and elasticity with which he springs from the ground is admirably expressed, as are also the playful pawings of the forelegs and the animated expression of lively impatience in the muscles and positions of the head and neck. Nor less to be admired are the form and character of the rider, the easy firmness of his seat, the perfect confidence in his own powers of command, his entire composure and tranquillity contrasted with the sudden and vehement action of the animal beneath him; and the grace and precision with which the whole framework of his body is indicated, and the muscular action developed."

PAGE 109. The monument of Dexileus, an Athenian knight, who was born, as the inscription shows, in 414 B. C., and who fell in battle near Corinth in 394. His youth may show that this was his first and last campaign. This monument is still *in situ* in the Street of Tombs, outside the Dipylon gate of Athens; near it are the stelae of others of the family of Dexileus. He is in the act of slaying a foeman. For the purposes of artistic effect he is not in armour. His weapon, whether sword or spear, and the bridle of his horse were doubtless added in bronze. From a photograph in my possession; the shadow at the left is caused by a wooden casing, set about the monument to preserve it. In the reproduction this casing is happily omitted.

PAGE 145. Assurbanipal (Sardanapalus), King of Assyria from 668 to 626 B. C., hunting wild asses. From a photograph of the alabaster relief found at Kouyunjik, Nineveh, now in the British

Museum. I have chosen this picture merely to illustrate the way in which the rein was attached to the bit, and the bridle to the branches (see p. 146). In the relief itself (though not in this reproduction) it is perfectly clear that the rein was fastened to the little ring.

ILLUSTRATIONS IN THE TEXT.

PAGE 13. From Panofka's " Bilder Antiker Lebens," iii, 1; he took it from Tischbein, "Vas d'Hamilton," i, 47. The painting represents the end of a race; the pillar indicating the goal. On the attachment of the bits, see p. 146. I have grave doubts about the trustworthiness of this picture, but insert it for its life and action. It must, if a correct reproduction, be a late work.

PAGE 19. Coin of King Patraos of Paeonia, 340-315 B. C. From a cut in "An Illustrated Dictionary to the Anabasis" by Professor J. W. White and the present writer, who took it from Baumeister, p. 2030. It is also illustrated and described by Imhoof-Blumer, "Monnaies Grecs," taf. c. The horseman, who is a Paeonian, wears trousers, and has an extremely large crest to his helmet. From his cuirass seems to rise the neckpiece (note 60, p. 151); note also the flaps about his loins (p. 66). The inscription above gives the king's name.

PAGE 20. Painting on an Attic vase now in Munich, found in the ancient Etruscan city of Vulci. From the "Archäologische Zeitung," xliii, taf. 11. The scene represents a riding-lesson, the old man at the right being the master. A young man rides along leading a second horse upon which his comrade is about to leap by the use of a vaulting-pole. For the sake of symmetry in the picture the artist may have placed this person in front of the horse instead of at the side, where he would naturally stand in taking such a leap; or it may be thought that he is merely balancing himself, ready to spring on as soon as the horse reaches him. When a cavalryman mounted by means of his spear, he used only one hand for the spear (see note 41, p. 139). Livy speaks of the use of the spear in leaping suddenly from a horse (iv, 19, 4). On the other half of this vase, not shown in my reproduction, a boy is leading a horse, while the teacher looks on under a tree, showing that this lesson was given in the open air. The riding-master Pheidon, mentioned in Mnesimachus's comedy of the "Horse-breeder," a work of the first half of the fourth century, gave his lessons in the agora, near the Hermae (see Athenaeus, 402 F.). But in another vase-painting (Daremberg et Saglio, ii, fig. 2717), young riders are exercising under cover. It is, therefore, impossible to say whether the ἱππασία mentioned by Xenophon at the end of his seventh chapter was in or out of doors. I have translated it riding-ground. In a different work (Memorabilia, iii, 3, 6), Xenophon calls the place ἄμμος (the Latin *harena*), showing that horses were exercised upon sand, not hard ground. The object hanging at the left of our picture is an oil-flask, perhaps the *aryballos* (see below), used in the baths and wrestling-schools. The inscription has nothing to do with the actual scene, but is an example of the custom whereby the ancient vase-painter dedicated, as it were, his work to some friend; to the name was generally attached the adjective καλός (handsome), as here. On the attachment of the horse's bit, see p. 146.

PAGE 22. A proto-Corinthian lecythos, of the shape sometimes called the *aryballos*, perhaps of the early sixth century. Athletes used such vases to hold their oil (see above). From "Die Griechischen Vasen," Lau, taf. iv, 2. The small size of the rider, compared to his horse, is noteworthy (see p. 95); observe also the thick, long mane (p. 94).

PAGE 23. From a vase found at Nola, in Campania; reproduced from Panofka's "Bilder Antiker Lebens," i, 5. A riding-master (see p. 168) is helping a boy to mount. In Plato, Laches, 182 A., riding is mentioned along with gymnastics as proper parts of the education of the

Athenian gentleman. In another place he says: "We must mount our children on horses in their earliest youth and take them on horseback to see war, in order that they may learn to ride; the horses must not be spirited and warlike, but the most tractable and yet the swiftest that can be had. In this way they will get an excellent view of what is hereafter to be their business; and if there is danger they have only to follow their elder leaders and escape" (Republic, 467 E, Jowett's translation). This heroic treatment, it must be remembered, is Plato's proposal for the ideal state, and it does not prove that boys were ever actually taken to see battles by the Athenians. The great physician Galen, of the second century A. D., advised that boys should begin to learn to ride at the age of seven (De val. tuend. i, 8; ii, 9). Such a boy seems to be represented in our picture. But probably in ancient Athens boys began to ride between the ages of fourteen and eighteen, which were the years especially devoted to training in gymnastics. At eighteen they were eligible for the cavalry, and began to learn to use weapons on horseback. This picture well illustrates the method of attaching the bit to the bridle (see p. 146).

PAGE 26. A coin of King Alexander of Macedon, 498-454 B. C., now in Berlin. From Baumeister, p. 950. Note the large size of the

ON THE ILLUSTRATIONS.   171

horse compared to the man (p. 98), his forelock (p. 32), and hogged mane (p. 91 ff.). I have already remarked on the extremely large branches of the bit (p. 148). The rider (a Macedonian of course) wears the short cloak adopted by the Athenian cavalry (p. 163), and the hat called *causia*, differing somewhat from the Athenian petasus (see p. 163). He carries two spears (p. 162).

PAGE 27. Painting on a black-figured vase in the British Museum, from Gerhard's "Auserlesene Vasenbilder," iv, 247. This is a Panathenaic vase, intended as a prize for the winner at the Panathenaic festival, probably at some time in the fourth century. This side of the vase shows the kind of contest for which the prize was given; on the other is the conventional figure of Athene. The rider in this case is not the owner, but a jockey. The owner's name is proclaimed by the man walking ahead, in the words ΔΥΝΕΙΚΕΤΥ: ΗΙΠΟΣ: ΝΙΚΑΙ, that is, "the horse of Dysnicetus is the winner." Behind walks a man carrying the prize, a tripod, on his head. In his left hand he holds a chaplet of victory; this, to my regret, is not shown in the present reproduction.

PAGE 29. A silver coin of Maronea in Thrace, 400–350 B. C. From Head's "Catalogue of the Greek Coins in the British Museum," Thrace, p. 126. This coin shows the leading-rein (note

38, p. 138). The inscription indicates the name of the town.

PAGE 30. From a black-figured amphora in the Hermitage collection, St. Petersburg, illustrated (in outline merely) in the "Comte Rendu de la Commission Impériale Archéologique," 1864, p. 5, from which I take it. The horse is bending his knees to allow the Amazon to mount (see p. 138). The inscription above has not been deciphered.

PAGE 33. From Koepp's "Ueber das Bildnis Alexanders des Grossen," p. 3. A gold medallion from Tarsus, of the time of the Emperor Commodus, in the "Cabinet des médailles," the obverse of which bears a fine head of Alexander the Great. The reverse, in our picture, shows the king hunting a lion. Professor Emerson has suggested (in the "American Journal of Archaeology," 1887, p. 253) that for this medallion was selected the central figures in a bronze group, called the Lion Hunt, by Lysippus, dedicated at Delphi by Craterus (Plutarch, Alexander, 40). In this group were included hunting-dogs and Craterus himself coming up to help. The picture shows the flaps at the shoulders and about the loins, mentioned by Xenophon in his description of the cuirass (p. 66). A leopard's skin serves instead of a cloth (notes 42, p. 140, and 66, p. 153). The inscription means "King Alexander."

PAGE 34. From Panofka's "Bilder Antiker

Lebens," iii, 7 (also in colours, a red-figured vase, in Gerhard's "Auserlesene Vasenbilder," iv, 272). The original, found at Vulci, Italy, is in the Royal Museum of Berlin. The picture shows the muzzle, the use of which is recommended by Xenophon whenever a horse is to be led (p. 31). The young man seems to be trying to avoid the difficulties in leading horses which Xenophon mentions (p. 35). He wears the regular cavalry boots (pp. 67 and 163). To the word ΕΓΡΑΦΣΕΝ, painted in the inscription, is prefixed (on the other side of the vase) the painter's name, Epictetus. On the word ΚΑΛΟΣ, see p. 169. Another picture, showing the muzzle in more detail, will be found in the "Jahrbuch des deutschen Arch. Instituts," 1889, taf. 10.

PAGE 38. A painting on a red-figured vase, somewhat broken, found at Orvieto, now in the Museo Egizio ed Etrusco, Florence; from the "Drittes Hallisches Winckelmannsprogramm," 1879, taf. iii, 2. The moon goddess, Selene, seated on a bridleless horse which is grazing or drinking. This goddess was first represented on horseback, so far as we know, by Phidias on the pedestal of the statue of Olympian Zeus (Pausanias, v, 11, 8). Other female divinities thus appearing in ancient art are Artemis, Aurora, and the Roman goddess of horses, Epona. But examples of mortal women on horseback are perhaps wanting in the art of Greece proper; not so in that of Asia (see for example the Heroon of Gjölbaschi, a work of the fifth century B. C., and Daremberg et Saglio, ii, p. 751). The Amazons, to be sure, are frequently found on horseback, riding like men; other females, whether goddesses or women, are represented as women ride to-day, except that, so far as I know, they are seated, not to the left, but to the right of the horse, as in our picture.

PAGE 39. Painting on a vase in the Berlin Museum, found probably at Nola; from the illustration in the " Archäologische Zeitung," 1878, taf. 22, where it is described by C. Robert. In this picture a young horseman (on his costume see p. 163) is making his horse throw forward the off forefoot so as to assume the position described by the verb ὑποβιβάζεσθαι (see p. 38 and note 37, p. 137). The motive of this picture and all the attitudes so closely resemble a group on the west side of the Parthenon frieze that Robert does not hesitate to say that the vase must have been painted in Athens, and that it is one of the rare instances of a vase-painting copied from work in stone. But Brunn, in an article in the same periodical (1880, p. 18) finds a similar motive in other works; for instance, in the coin of Larissa (see p. 54 of this book) and in a Roman relief (mentioned on p. 138). He concludes that this

ON THE ILLUSTRATIONS. 175

was a typical position seen in every riding-school, and hence that there is no proof that our picture was painted in Athens or copied from the Parthenon. Note the method of attachment of the bit (p. 146), and the leading-rein, distinguished from the bridle-rein (p. 163). On the fetlocks, see note 6, p. 122.

PAGE 44. A statuette found in the excavations at Dodona, the ancient seat of the worship of Zeus. It is of the most archaic style of work found there, and may belong to the seventh century B. C. I take the picture from " Dodone et ses ruines," Carapanos, pl. 13, 1, described in vol. i, p. 183. The mane of the horse is very thick and long (see p. 91); the forelock is arranged in a sort of tuft, as in Assyrian reliefs (see for example the plate facing p. 145). A similar arrangement, though not found, I believe, in works of the fifth and early fourth century, appears again in later art; see the frontispiece of this book, and the cuts on pp. 13 and 51. On the bridle, see p. 146. The peculiar shape of the rein (I mean the swallow-tailed look at the middle) is found in some Assyrian reliefs; and on the whole this statuette bears many resemblances to those works.

PAGE 45. From "Peintures de Vases Antiques recueilles par Millin et Millingen: publiés et commentées par S. Reinach," pl. i, 45. A vase in the Malmaison collection in the Louvre, found in

Southern Italy. The scene represents a contest at the Panathenaic festival. This contest is referred to in an Attic inscription of the first part of the fourth century (C. I. A., ii, 965). A shield was set up, and at it riders hurled the javelin while passing at full gallop. In our picture the first rider has already thrown his javelin, which has broken against the shield and lies on the ground; the rider is soothing his horse by the means employed also on the Parthenon frieze (see the end of note 46, p. 143). The second rider is about to hurl his javelin, and the winged figures above with crown and fillets indicate that he is to be the winner. This game originated at Argos, at the festival of Hera; and the shield went to the winner (Pindar, Ol. 7, 83; Nem. 10, 22; Hyginus, 170, 273). On the bits, see p. 146.

PAGE 50. A bit found on the Acropolis of Athens, fully described in note 53, p. 145.

PAGE 51. Bronze statuette found at Herculaneum in 1761. From an engraving in Duruy's "Histoire des Grecs," iii, p. 233, where it is taken from a photograph. It is also given, in outline, in the Museo Borbonico, iii, tav. 27. Now in the Naples Museum. Save in the mane and tail, this horse corresponds closely to the description of Simon (p. 107 ff.).

PAGE 54. A silver coin of Larissa, in Thessaly; from the "Monatsberichte der Königlichen Preussischen Akad. der Wiss.," 1878, taf. 2, 30. Of the motive, as Brunn understands it, I have spoken already (p. 174). On the costume of the man, see p. 163. The inscription gives the name of the place.

PAGE 55. From an engraving in "Schliemann's Excavations," Schuchhardt, translated by Sellers, p. 132. A fragment of a vase found in the excavations at Tiryns, and perhaps of the ninth or tenth century B.C. The animals and the men all have a wooden look; but in spite of the stiff legs, flat belly, huge eyes, and flame-like mane of the horse, yet the shape of the head and neck of the horse show that even in this, the most archaic of the pictures in this book, the artist had before his mind the type of animal which we see in the best art (see p. 90). The lines above the horse's back are not intended for reins, but are part of the geometrical ornamentation. The men carry each a shield and a spear, and probably wore the skin of some animal of which the tail appears dangling down below. The colouring of this vase is a lustrous brown on a light yellow ground.

PAGE 60. A bit, fully described on p. 147.

PAGE 61. From Schoene's "Griechische Reliefs," taf. 17. Part of the fragment of a relief found in Attica, now in the Pinakothek, Munich. The lower part, here omitted, contains an olive crown, showing that the relief was set up by a victor in a ἱππικὸς ἀγών or πομπή, an equestrian contest or a parade; perhaps he was a hipparch or phylarch (see p. 75). I have chosen this relief because it seems to illustrate Xenophon's words on the proper way to lead a troop of cavalry, if you wish to make the whole line "a sight well worth seeing" (p. 64).

PAGE 64. A silver coin of Ichnae, in Macedonia, 500–480 B. C. From the "Catalogue of the Greek Coins in the British Museum," Macedonia, p. 76. Note the hogged mane of the horse (p. 94) and the rider's greaves (note 63, p. 153). The inscription gives the name of the town.

PAGE 65. An Attic black-figured vase of the fifth century; from Gerhard's "Vases Étrusques et Campaniens du Mus. Roy. de Berlin," pl. xii. The horsemen wear greaves (note 63, p. 153), and each carries two spears (p. 162); the helmet may be the type called Boeotian (note 61, p. 152). The inscriptions at the left and at the right show that the two men are the Attic heroes, Acamas and Demophon, sons of Theseus and Phaedra. Homer does not mention them; but according to later stories current among the Athenians, they went to the Trojan war, and Vergil puts Acamas among the heroes in the Trojan horse. They appear several times in vase-paintings; and there were bronze equestrian statues of them on the Acropolis, as well as a painting of them by Polygnotus at Delphi. The names of their horses are

ON THE ILLUSTRATIONS. 179

given in our picture, — Phalius, of the horse at the left, and Calliphora, of that at the right. The first, which was also the name of the charger of Belisarius (Procopius, B. G. i, 18), means that the animal had a white star on his forehead; the second means "handsome legged." The perpendicular inscription between the two animals is a dedication (see p. 169) of the vase to the handsome Onetorides.

PAGE 69. Bronze statuette of Alexander on Bucephalas in the Naples Museum, found at Herculaneum; from the outline engraving in the "Museo Borbonico," iii, 43. Ever since its discovery in 1761, it has been supposed to be a reduced copy from the bronze group by Lysippus, made at Alexander's own order, to represent an incident at the battle on the Granicus in 334 B. C. In this battle the king's helmet was broken by a blow from a sword (Plutarch, Alex. 17); hence he is here represented bare-headed. The entire group, consisting of many figures, was carried to Rome by Metellus (Vell. Pat. i, 11, 3). This horse closely resembles the other (p. 51) found at the same time and place. On the broad brow, see note 12, p. 125; on the cloth, note 42, p. 140; on the bit, p. 149; on the breastplate, p. 67; on the flaps at Alexander's shoulders and loins, p. 66.

PAGE 106. From an engraving in "Antiquités de Bosphore Cimmérien," Reinach, pl. xx. A repoussé gold ornament, here represented a little more than half the size of the original, found in Koul-Oba in the Crimea, now in St. Petersburg. The scene represents a Scythian horseman hunting a hare. On the bit, see p. 146.

PAGE 107. From "Monuments Grecs publiés par l'association pour l'encouragement des études Grecques en France," Nos. 14–16, pl. 5, with a long description. The vase, found at Vulci in Etruria, is now in the Louvre, and was made in Athens, probably about 450 B. C. Our picture, which is painted on the inside of the cup, represents a young cavalryman with curled hair, through which is passed a red fillet. He wears a long mantle, richly made and of some rather stiff material, instead of the usual short cloak (pp. 163, 171); his petasus (p. 163) is hanging at his back by a cord which passes round his neck; another cord hanging on his shoulder served to keep the hat in place when it was worn on the head. His boots are of the usual cavalry pattern (p. 163), and he carries two javelins (p. 162). The horse is decidedly ugly; he is too thin and bony, and his head is too long and narrow at the sides to satisfy a Greek connoisseur. Yet the artist has not done badly with the details of the anatomy, the muscles of the back and hind quarters, the folds where the fore legs are set on, and with the tail. The bridle is merely indicated, but we can see how the bit was attached (p. 146). The pose of horse and man being one of complete repose, it may be thought that we have here an outpost, doing guard duty, — perhaps in winter, as this might account for the heavy cloak. A good list of vase-paintings of men on horseback will be found in the article from which I have taken the above description.

PAGE 119. From Engelmann and Anderson's "Pictorial Atlas to Homer," plate xiv, 74. From a Panathenaic vase (see p. 171) of the sixth century B. C., found at Camirus in Rhodes. It is better illustrated in Salzmann's "Nécropole de Camiros," pl. 57, as black-figured on an orange ground. The scene represents acrobats performing, and I take the following description from the first book named above: "Two horses are in full gallop in the ring, guided by a single rider, who looks round at an acrobat, who, with the aid of a spring-board, has leaped on the back of his horse, and, with two shields, is performing a martial dance, jumping from one to the other. He is represented as very small on account of the lack of space. Below, between the horses' legs, is another figure (also made small and placed in this strange position for want of space) who is busily engaged in smoothing the sand of the ring with a pick, just as the grooms do with a rake in the modern circus. Behind the horses is a man playing on a double flute in front of the spectators, who are seated on tiers of benches to the left. They are applauding loudly, and one of them shouts, ' Bravo, fine tumbling!' (καλῶς τοι κυβιστεῖτοι). On the right a youth is seen climbing up a pole (with a slanting support at one side); but whether this is another performance or part of the jockey's display, it is impossible to determine."

Although we have no evidence of riding in the Heroic age, as I have remarked above (p. 74 and note 71, p. 154), yet at the time when the Homeric poems were composed, riding had reached such a stage of progress that even acrobatic performances on horseback were not unknown. One of the Homeric similes to which I referred in the note just mentioned runs as follows: "As when a man that well knows how to ride, harnesses up four chosen horses, and, springing from the ground, dashes to the great city along the public highway; and crowds of men and women look on in wonder; while he with all confidence, as his steeds fly on, keeps leaping from one to another" (Iliad, xv, 679 ff.). Scenes like the one portrayed in our picture were probably familiar to the writer of those verses. This performance seems to be taking place in a regular circus. What has been called a "spring-board" in the description above quoted seems to me to be almost exactly like one of those hollow wooden pedestals on which the helpers in the modern circus stand when they hold out the paper hoops through which the rider is to jump. Of an event in which highly trained horses bore a part an amusing story is told. The luxurious people of Sybaris in Southern Italy had trained their horses to dance to the music of the flute. Their inveterate enemies, the people of Croton, took advantage of this, and having substituted flutes instead of the usual trumpets in their army, suddenly struck up a dancing tune just as a battle was beginning. Thereupon the horses of the Sybarites instantly threw off their riders, and began to skip and dance, and the men of Croton won the battle (Aelian, N. A., xvi, 23). If there is any truth in this story, it shows either that the Greeks of Magna Graecia used cavalry earlier than the people of Greece proper (for Sybaris was destroyed by Croton in 510 B. C., and we have seen that the Athenians had no cavalry before the Persian wars), or else that the event described took place after the return of the Sybarites to the site of their old city, about 450 B. C.

PAGE 157. A silver coin of Potidaea, of about 500 B. C., from the "Catalogue of Coins in the British Museum," Macedonia, p. 99. The rider is Poseidon Hippios, the sea-god here appearing as patron of horses, which, according to the myth, he created. On the size of the horse see p. 98.

PAGE 159. From an amphora illustrated and described in the "Achtes Hallisches Winckelmannsprogramm," 1883. The vase is of the middle of the third century B. C., was found at Ruvi in Apulia, and is now in the Naples Museum. I have taken from it only the figure of a Greek warrior; in the rest of the picture an Eastern king is escaping from him at full speed in a chariot. It is thought that the painting, without referring to any actual historical scene, symbolizes the triumph of Alexander, as representing Greek civilization, over Darius, as the representative of the East.

TAILPIECE. A silver coin of King Pausanias of Macedon, 390–389 B. C., from the "Catalogue of Greek Coins in the British Museum," Macedonia, p. 169. I have spoken above (note 72, p. 155) of the letter Koppa branded upon horses of extraordinary value. On the hindquarter of this horse is branded a caduceus, or staff of Hermes. Other brands are mentioned in Daremberg et Saglio, ii, p. 800. The inscription on this coin gives the king's name.

INDEX.

ACHILLES, horses of, 99, 156.
Acrobats, 181 ff.
Action of the horse, 55, 59, 117.
Age of horses, 17, 23, 127.
Alexander the Great, 101 ff.; in art, 172, 179, 184.
Amble, the, 141.
Apelles, 84, 106.
Apsyrtus on the horse, 86, 115.
Arm, piece of armour called the, 66, 152.
Armour for the horse, 67, 153; for the rider, 65 ff., 67 ff.
Assurbanipal, portrait of, 166.

BACK, double, 17, 112, 113, 114, 115, 125.
Back sinew, 16, 109, 123.
Bareback riding, 41.
Barley surfeit, 28, 128.
Barrel, the, 88, 111, 114, 116.
Bars, the, 124.
Bit, the, 36, 53, 138, 144 ff.; branches of the, 148, 161, 171; flexible, 57, 58; in art, 160, 163, 167, 170, 175, 179; rough, 57, 144 ff.; smooth, 56, 144 ff.; stiff, 57, 58, 149.
Bits, kinds of, 56, 144 ff.
Boots, for the rider, 67, 154; in art, 163, 165, 173, 180.
Branches of the bit, 148; in art, 161, 171.
Brands on horses, 72; in art, 184.
Breaking, 20.
Breastplate, for the horse, 67; in art, 179.

Breeds of horses, 78.
Bridle. *See* Bit.
Bridling, 35.
Brood mares, 32, 117, 135.
Bucephalas, 78, 101 ff., 125; in art, 179.
Bucephalus type, 101, 125; in art, 160, 165, 179.

CALPURNIUS on the horse, 86, 112.
Career, the, 43, 79.
Causia, in art, 171.
Cavalry, Athenian, 20, 75 f.; in art, 162; dress of, in art, 103; examination for, 76, 173.
Cheek-piece, 146.
Chest of the horse, 16, 109, 111, 113, 114, 115.
China eye, 102.
Chin-strap, 39, 136.
Chirrup, 55, 144.
Chlamys, in art, 163, 180.
Cloth, the, 41, 67, 140, 154; in art, 172, 179.
Cluck, 55, 144.
Colour of the horse, 108, 112, 117.
Columella on the horse, 86, 112.
Coronet, the, 113, 116.
Cropping, 134.
Cuirass, 65, 150; in art, 165.
Curb, 80, 144.
Curry-comb, 133.

DEMI-PESADE, 79, 126, 150.
Dexileus, monument of, 166.
Discs on the bit, 56, 145.

INDEX.

Diseases of the horse, 28.
Dismounting, 44, 168.
Docking, 134.
δοκιμασια, 76; in art, 163 f.
Driving, 74.

EARS of the horse, 17, 109, 111, 112, 114, 115, 117, 125.
Echini on the bit, 56, 145.
εχῖνος, 145.
Eleusinion, 13, 120.
Examination for the cavalry, 75; in art, 163 ff.
Eyes of the horse, 17, 109, 111, 112, 115, 117; china, 102.

FEED, 128.
Feet of the horse, 14, 28, 116.
Fetlocks, 15, 109, 122; in art, 175.
Flaps on the cuirass, 66, 151; in art, 167, 172, 179.
Forearms, 16, 115, 124.
Forelock, 32, 113; in art, 164, 171, 175.
Frog, the, 15, 29, 34, 115, 122.
Frontlet, 67.

GAITS of the horse, 42, 59, 63, 79, 97, 141, in art, 141, 163, 164.
Gallop, the, 141.
Geldings, 98.
Girth, 140.
γνωμονες, 120.
Greaves, 66, 153; in art, 178.
Grooming, 31, 34, 133.

HALTER, 30, 31, 39.
Hands, the, 42, 53, 56.
Head of the horse, 32, 109, 111, 112, 113, 115, 117, 124.
Headpiece, 36, 136.
Headstall, 36, 136.
Helmet, the, 66, 152; in art, 165, 178.
Hipparch, 75, 164, 178.
Hogging, 93.
Hoofs, 15, 28, 108, 111, 112, 113, 114, 115, 116, 117.

Horace on the horse, 120.
Horse, armour not Greek, 153; an expensive animal, 76 ff.; in art, 81 ff., 158 ff.; high-mettled, the, 52; introduction in Greece, 155, nature of the, 98; primarily used for war, 100; type of, how determined, 90; writers on the, 86 ff. *See also* Breaking, Colour, Gaits, Head, Hoofs, Mane, Points, Size, etc.
Horse-raising, 78.
Horse-shoes, 121.
Horses, dancing, 183.
Hunting, 48, 143.
ὑπόβασις, 126.
υποβιβαζομαι, 137, 174.

JAVELIN game, 176.
Javelins, 48, 68; in art, 161, 164.
Jaws of the horse, 17, 109.

KNEES of the horse, 16, 111, 113, 115.
Koppa horse, 155, 184.

LEADING-REIN, 35, 136, 138; in art, 163, 171, 173, 175.
Leads, the, 42, 140.
Leaping, 46.
Loin of the horse, 17, 61, 110, 150.

MANE, the, 32, 47, 81, 91 ff., 108, 111, 112, 113, 114, 115, 117, 135, 156; in art, 164, 169, 170, 175, 178.
Mares. *See* Brood mares.
Markers, 23, 126.
Marks in the teeth, 127.
Mash, 128
Micon, 85.
Milk-teeth, 126.
Mounting, 37, 38, 39 f., 52, 104, 136, 137, 139; in art, 168, 172, 174.
Mounting-blocks, 139.
Mouth of the horse, 29.
Muzzle, 31, 131; in art, 173.

INDEX.

NAMES of horses, 179.
Nature of the horse, 98.
Neck of the horse, 16, 109, 112, 114, 115, 117.
Neck-piece, 65, 151, in art, 167.
Nemesian on the horse, 86, 114.
Nicking, 134.
Nose-band, 39, 136, 139.
Nostrils, 17, 109, 111, 112, 113, 115, 117, 124.

ὀκλάζειν, 138, 172.
Oppian on the horse, 86, 113.

PACE, the, 141.
Palladius on the horse, 87, 116.
Parthenon horses, 79, 83, 89, 94, 95, 97, 138, 143, 149, 151, 160, 165.
Pasterns, 109, 114.
Pauson, 84.
πέδη, 127.
Pelagonius, 86, 115.
περόνη, 122.
Petasus, 163, 171, 180.
Phidias, 83.
Phylarch, 75; in art, 164, 178.
Pliny on the horse, 89.
Points of the horse, 80 ff., 87, 107 ff.
Poise, the, 24.
Poll, the, 16, 17, 109.
Pollux on the horse, 91, 156.
Prices of horses, 76, 102.

QUARTERS, the, 18.

RACING, 75, 171.
Rearing, 61, 63.
Reins, 42, 161.
Riding, 74 ff.; acrobatic, 181 ff.; age for learning, 170; not in Heroic age, 74, 154, 182; in Homer, 74, 182; later than driving, 74; never for pleasure, 100.
Riding-boots. See Boots.
Riding-masters, 79, 168, 169.
Riding-school, 168.
Rings on the bit, 57, 149.

SABRE, 67.
Saddle, 80, 140. See Cloth.
Schlieben on the horse, 80, 81, 87, 91.
Scythian bowmen, 164.
Seat, the, 40, 48.
Selene, horse of, 165; on horseback, 173.
Shanks, the, 15, 18, 109, 111, 113, 115, 126.
Shoes, 121.
Shying, 37.
Simon, 13, 15, 62, 79, 85, 86, 107, 119, 176.
Size of the horse, 18, 95, 126, 139, 169, 170, 183.
Snaffle, twisted, 146.
Solea, 121.
Spear, 68.
Spurs, 46, 142.
Stable, 27, 128.
Stall, the, 28, 128.
Stallions, 98, 116.
Stirrups, 80, 137.
Stonehenge on the horse, 89.
Stones in stalls, 28, 128.
Sword, 154.

TAIL of the horse, 32, 110, 113, 114, 115, 116, 117.
Teeth of the horse, 109, 110, 126.
τροχοί, 145.
Trot, the, 141.

VARRO on the horse, 86, 111.
Veins in the horse, 111.
Vergil on the horse, 86, 111.
Volte, the, 24, 43, 79, 127.

WALK, the, 141.
Washing, 32, 33.
Withers, the, 17, 110, 111.
Women riding, 173

XENOPHON, his life, 70 ff.

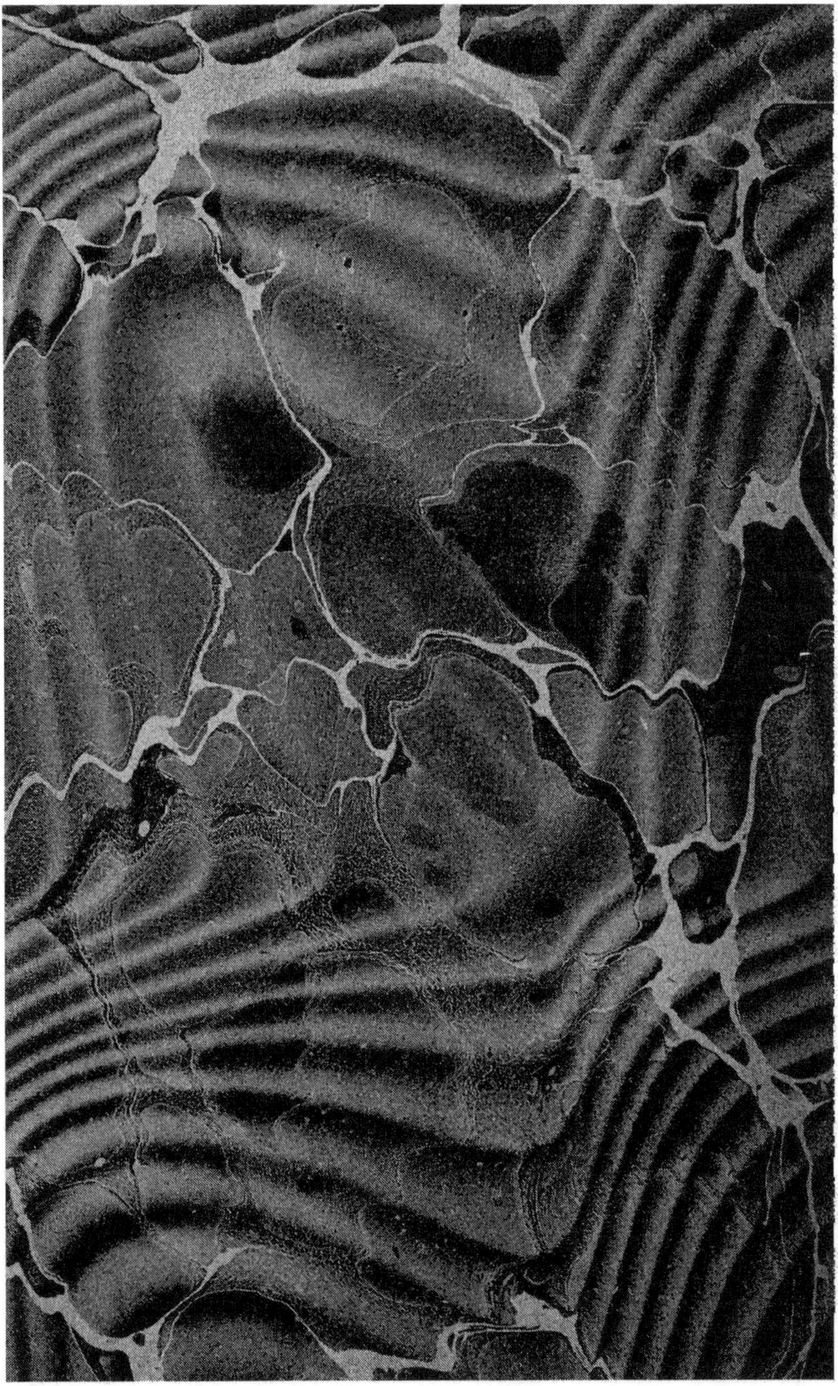

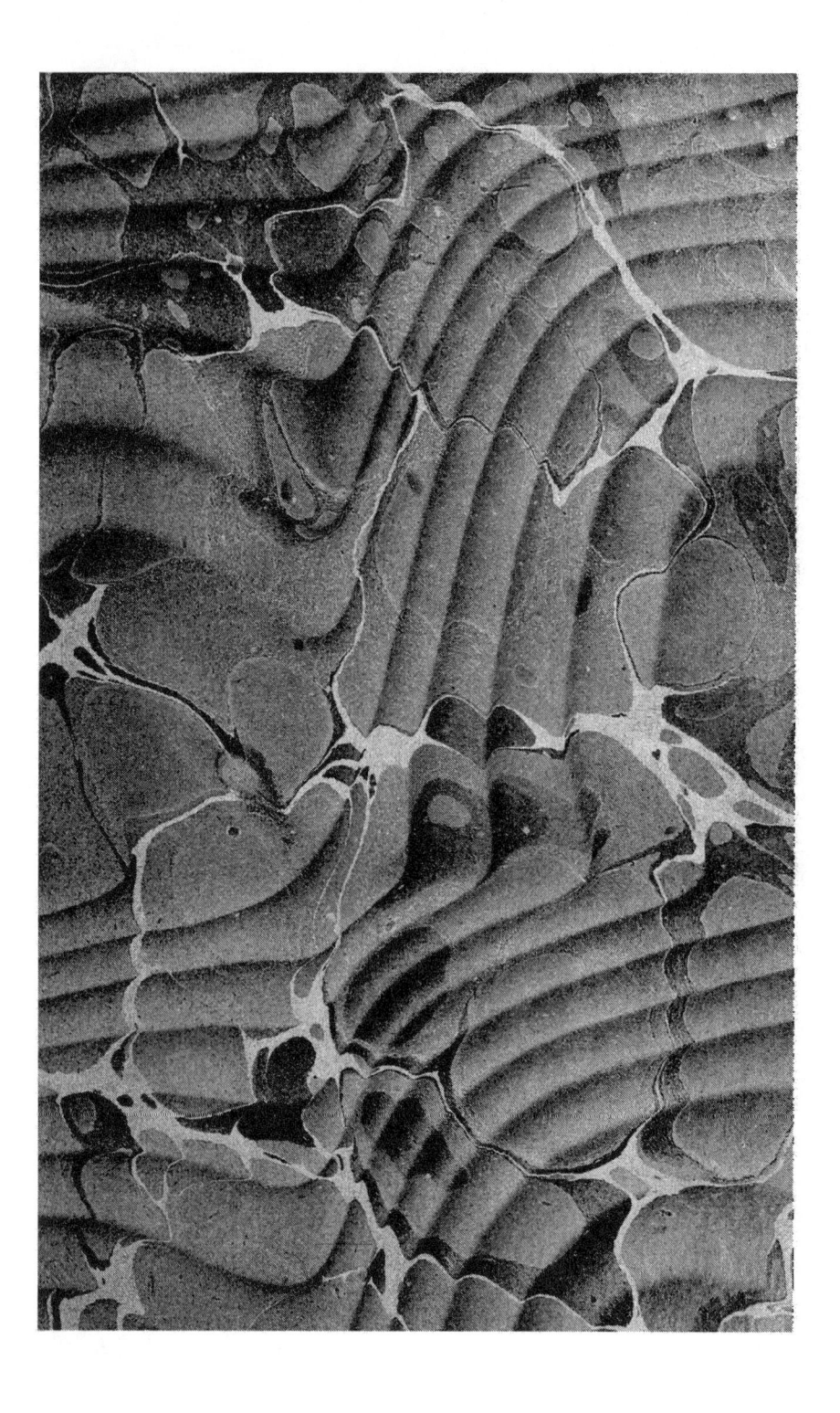

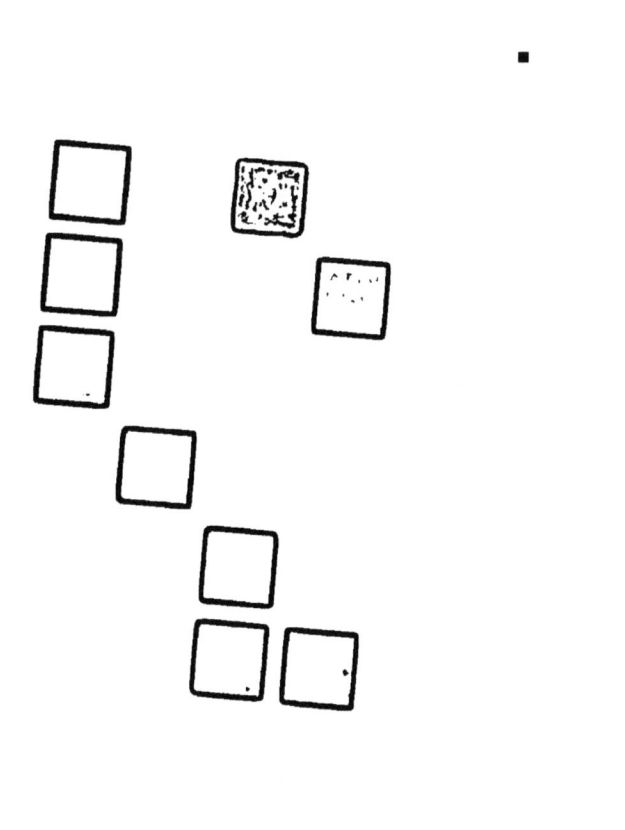

CPSIA information can be obtained
at www.ICGtesting.com
Printed in the USA
LVHW09*1314070818
586238LV00006B/39/P

Would You Rather...?

Over **300** Fabulously Feminine Dilemmas to Ponder

for WOMEN

by Diane Bullock & M. Schuster

Edited by Justin Heimberg & David Gomberg

Published by Seven Footer Press
267 Fifth Avenue, Suite 301
New York, NY 10001

First Printing, February 2009
10 9 8 7 6 5 4 3 2

© Copyright Justin Heimberg and David Gomberg, 2009
All Rights Reserved

Would you rather...?® is a registered trademark owned by Falls Media LLC

Design by Tom Schirtz

ISBN-13 978-1-934734-22-3

Without limiting the rights under copyright reserved above, no parts of this publication may be reproduced, stored in or introduced into a retrieval system, or transmitted in any form, or by any means (electronic, mechanical, photocopying, recording or otherwise), without the prior written permission of both the copyright owner and the above publisher of this book.

www.wouldyourather.com / www.sevenfooter.com

How To Use This Book

Sit around with a bunch of friends and read a question aloud, discussing it until the momentum of the conversation fades into awkward silence and nervous glances. Everybody must choose. As the Deity proclaims, **YOU MUST CHOOSE!** That's the whole premise of this thing. It forces you to really think about the options. Once everyone has chosen, move on to the next question. It's that simple. We have provided a few things to consider when deliberating each question, but don't restrict yourself to these topics, as much of the fun comes from imagining the different ways your choice will affect your life.

Tough Choices

They say that it's hard out there for a pimp. Long hours, sore backhand, velvet rash. But what most Oscar winning songs don't mention is the grueling and time-consuming life of the modern woman.

The new millennium has ushered in a progressive mantra: gender equality. Sure, women's rights are questioned and contested worldwide and a male commuter would sooner oggle your rack before he gave up his seat on the subway. Granted, Hollywood continues to glorify matrimony and childbirth remains a standard rite for women. OK. And there's still a significant disparity in average pay between the sexes. Fine.

But, uh... what was... Oh yeah! Equality! Right. There's a whole mess of that. And with equality comes choice. With choice comes great power. With great power comes great responsibility. But let's focus on choice.

Would you rather buckle down and focus on a career, or nab a nice guy and start a family? Would you rather spend your savings on a new wardrobe and a hypoallergenic cat, or invest it in corduroy futures? Heels or flats? Paper or plastic? IUD or cervical cap?

The world supplies you with an endless amount of choices and, as a woman, your life and your gender depend on prudent and measured responses to shape a dignified future not just for women, but for humanity as we know it.

Of course, the choices aren't always easy…

Table of Contents

Sex 1

Beauty & Fashion 33

Celebrities & Pop Culture 69

Powers & Fantasies 95

Weird, Gross, Embarrassing & Painful 123

Workin' 9 to 5(ish) 163

More Sex 181

Random Play 205

CHAPTER 1

SEX

These are the circumstances. A powerful deity descends from on high and informs you that, for reasons beyond your understanding, your sex life is about to change. The Deity bestows upon you a choice between two sexually-charged fates. "Neither" is not an option. **You must choose!**

Would you rather...

your orgasm be as loud as a howler monkey

OR

as gushing as Mentos dropped in Diet Coke?

Would you rather...

have your ex come crawling back

OR

have your ex crawl, literally, for the rest of his life?

YOU MUST CHOOSE!

Would you rather have sex with...

Johnny Depp **OR** Brad Pitt?

50 Cent **OR** Dr. Drew?

Matthew Fox **OR** Jake Gyllenhaal?

Jimmy Kimmel **OR** Mitt Romney?

A first cousin of your choice **OR** John Madden?

YOU MUST CHOOSE!

Would you rather...

have your wedding videographer be Joe Francis (creator of *Girls Gone Wild*)

OR

have your wedding ceremony officiated by Flavor Flav?

Things to consider: Flav's gift for words, your great aunt's affinity for beads, who would go wild?

YOU MUST CHOOSE!

Would you rather...
have "innie" nipples

OR
a horizontal vagina?

Things to consider: nude beaches, getting naked for the first time

Would you rather...
have your boobs drop six inches overnight

OR
have your butt drop six inches overnight?

YOU MUST CHOOSE!

Would you rather...

never fight with your boyfriend/husband

OR

fight once a week and have great make-up sex?

Would you rather...

have a compulsion that causes you to invariably refer to your breasts as "my jiggle set"

OR

always refer to your vagina as "my love canyon"?

Things to consider: doctor's appointments, writing love letters, getting work at *Penthouse*

YOU MUST CHOOSE!

Would you rather...

on your wedding day, accidentally say an old boyfriend's name during your vows

OR

after walking down the aisle to make your entrance, realize you have skidmarks on your wedding dress?

YOU MUST CHOOSE!

Would you rather have a lesbian encounter with...

Angelina Jolie **OR** Megan Fox?

Halle Berry **OR** Heidi Klum?

Reese Witherspoon **OR** Elisabeth Hasselbeck?

Lassie **OR** Rosie O'Donnell?

YOU MUST CHOOSE!

Would you rather...

have the ability to instantly make your breasts the size of your choice

OR

have a butt capable of altering size and shape to fit into any pair of pants (but only while you are wearing the pants)?

Things to consider: disrobing for sex, jogging

YOU MUST CHOOSE!

Would you rather your sex partner have...

a one-inch penis

OR

the most perfect penis; however it's jutting out of his lower back? His neck? The bottom of his left foot?

Would you rather...

have a Crazy Straw clitoris

OR

three butt cheeks?

Things to consider: finding jeans that fit, zipper snags

YOU MUST CHOOSE!

Would you rather...

receive an email alert every time your boyfriend thinks of having sex with another woman

OR

not?

YOU MUST CHOOSE!

Would you rather...

fellate a guy with a 14-inch penis while you're suffering from a sore throat

OR

receive anal sex from a guy with a 2-inch diameter penis?

Would you rather...

passionately make out with a heavy drooler

OR

give oral sex to a heavy farter?

YOU MUST CHOOSE!

Would you rather...

have genitalia that whistles like a tea pot when you get turned on

OR

genitalia that emits a loud buzz and flashes a *Family Feud* "X" when you're turned off?

YOU MUST CHOOSE!

Would you rather your partner...

always remember your anniversary but never buy you a gift

OR

never remember your anniversary but always buy you a lavish "I'm sorry" gift?

Would you rather...

have the sounds of your love-making uploaded everyday on iTunes

OR

have a video of you in the throes of masturbation posted on YouTube?

YOU MUST CHOOSE!

Would you rather...

at bars, constantly be hit on by every guy no matter how lame he is

OR

always have to make the first move?

Sex

YOU MUST CHOOSE!

Would you rather...

your naked body appear to be rippling like it's in a wind tunnel

OR

your naked body have banners reading "OUTRAGEOUS!!!" obscuring your crotch and breasts?

YOU MUST CHOOSE!

Would you rather date someone...

with a perfect face **OR** a 9-inch penis?

with a 2-inch wide, 3-inch long penis **OR** a half-inch wide, 10-inch long penis?

with a ribbed-for-your-pleasure penis **OR** a snake tongue?

YOU MUST CHOOSE!

Would you rather...

be able to achieve orgasm with no physical stimulus (just thought and emotion)

OR

be able to achieve orgasm from purely physical stimulation (thought and emotion are irrelevant)?

YOU MUST CHOOSE!

Would you rather be forced to always have sex...

to the soundtrack of *High School Musical* **OR** festive Indian music?

in strobe light **OR** with NASCAR airing in the background?

in libraries **OR** janitorial closets?

YOU MUST CHOOSE!

Would you rather...

have sex with Mel Gibson **OR** Kevin Federline?

John Mayer **OR** Ryan Reynolds?

Josh Groban **OR** Kanye West?

the character of Dr. House **OR** the character of Chuck from *Gossip Girl*?

a sea lion **OR** Dick Cheney?

YOU MUST CHOOSE!

Would you rather have all of your sex dreams directed by...

Jerry Bruckheimer **OR** Judd Apatow?

the Wachowski brothers **OR** the Coen brothers?

David Lynch **OR** Pixar?

Sex

YOU MUST CHOOSE!

Would you rather only have sex...

standing up

OR

without ever facing one another?

Would you rather...

have no vagina

OR

have 17 vaginas all over your body?

Things to consider: porn career, dealing with constant menstrual cycles would be like being a plate-spinner (or would the cycles align?)

YOU MUST CHOOSE!

Would you rather...

have to find your husband in the Craigslist "Casual Encounters" section

OR

have your selection for a husband limited to people on *Celebrity Rehab*?

YOU MUST CHOOSE!

Would you rather be thought of as...

"chunky" **OR** "frumpy"?

"humorless" **OR** "shrill"?

"plain" **OR** "handsome"?

YOU MUST CHOOSE!

Would you rather...

marry and take the name of Derrick Fingerblast

OR

Ronald Queefcloud?

Things to Consider: playing the Native American card

Would you rather...

tattoo Bret Michaels's name on your forehead

OR

have unprotected sex with him and just hope for the best?

YOU MUST CHOOSE!

Would you rather...

be able to blow visible kisses across a room

OR

be able to fart directionally with an accuracy of 40 feet?

Date, Marry, or Screw?

Tom Cruise, Johnny Depp, Barack Obama

Anderson Cooper, the Pick-Up Artist, Seth Rogen

Mike Huckabee, Tom Colicchio, The Incredible Hulk

YOU MUST CHOOSE!

Would you... never send another text message to have sex with George Clooney?

Would you... eat your next 50 meals at McDonald's to grope Justin Timberlake?

Would you... have your breasts surgically altered so that one was a B-cup and the other was a DDD-cup to have Josh Hartnett as a sex slave?

YOU MUST CHOOSE!

Would you ever have sex...

in a dressing room stall at the mall?

in a car in a public parking lot?

in your parents' bed?

in a Foot Locker with both of you wearing referee shirts?

in Narnia?

YOU MUST CHOOSE!

Would you rather...

have a three-way with Jordin Sparks and Clay Aiken **OR** David Archuleta and Kelly Clarkson?

Ryan Gosling and Michael Phelps **OR** Shia LaBeouf and Gerard Butler?

Nelly Furtado and Kid Rock **OR** Petra Nemcova and Urkel (in character)?

Sarah Palin and John McCain **OR** Barack Obama and Hillary Clinton?

YOU MUST CHOOSE!

Would you rather...

come home to find your partner cheating on you

OR

wake up in the middle of the night to find your partner online and masturbating to Chris Crocker
(the "Leave Britney Alone" guy)?

Would you... make an agreement with your boyfriend or husband to allow each other 3 celebrities where infidelity would be permitted?
If so, who would each of you pick?

YOU MUST CHOOSE!

Would you rather find your parents reading...

your diary

OR

The Kama Sutra?

Would you rather...

have sex with Ben Affleck if he gained 50 pounds

OR

Ashton Kutcher if was speaking the entire time?

YOU MUST CHOOSE!

CHAPTER 2

Beauty & Fashion

In a steadfast refusal to reach for the remote, the Deity has resigned himself to watching Bravo for the remainder of the afternoon. Though infuriated by the shrill entitlement of guest judges, the Deity has to give them credit: That hemline was inappropriate for a formal affair. With wardrobes and physical appearances on his mind, the Deity commands you to select between two choices that might severely alter the way you sashay down the runway.

Would you rather...

have perpetual camel toe

OR

perpetual uni-boob?

Would you rather...

be able to buy only two new pairs of shoes a year

OR

be able to buy as many shoes as you want,
but only one shoe of each pair?

YOU MUST CHOOSE!

Would you rather always...

be on the tail-end of every fashion trend

OR

be 20 years ahead of every trend?

Things to consider: the silver vest craze of 2030

Beauty & Fashion

YOU MUST CHOOSE!

Would you rather have a different one-of-a-kind outfit designed for you every day by...

Christian Siriano **OR** Zac Posen?

Ralph Lauren **OR** Vivienne Westwood?

Marc Jacobs **OR** Stella McCartney?

Things to consider: Who would you choose as your personal designer?

YOU MUST CHOOSE!

Would you rather...

get a face lift on only the left side of your face
OR
inject your eyelids with lots of collagen?

Beauty & Fashion

YOU MUST CHOOSE!

Would you rather...

be limited to wearing Tevas and socks for footwear

OR

only be able to use a plastic Walgreen's bag as a purse?

YOU MUST CHOOSE!

Would you rather all your weight go...

to your thighs **OR** to your butt?

to your stomach **OR** to your ankles and upper arms?

to your neck **OR** to your forehead?

Beauty & Fashion

YOU MUST CHOOSE!

Would you rather...

have a "tramp stamp"

OR

"taint paint"?

YOU MUST CHOOSE!

Would you rather...

be limited to a half pound of clothing every day

OR

have to wear no less than 30 pounds of jewelry?

Things to consider: exercising at the gym, cold days

YOU MUST CHOOSE!

Would you rather...

be on *Project Runway*

OR

have your significant other go on *What Not to Wear?*

Would you rather...

receive every haircut from a non-English speaking stylist at Supercuts

OR

have your wardrobe consist exclusively of Dress Barn hand-me-downs?

YOU MUST CHOOSE!

Would you rather...

have copious amounts of areola hair

OR

a "happy trail" that reached your neck?

Would you rather...

have to wear a four pound nipple piercing
OR
have to wear a four-inch diameter clitoral hoop earring?
Things to consider: wearing tight clothing, snags

Would you...

pay an additional 20% income tax for the rest of your life if you could give all your weight gain to another person of your choosing?

YOU MUST CHOOSE!

Would you rather always have to wear...

Brillo undies **OR** furry Russian hats?

an iridescent blue lace and satin bridesmaid dress with matching parasol **OR** Bjork's swan dress?

a "SLUT" T-shirt **OR** an "ISO Free Mustache Rides" button?
Things to consider: job interviews, first dates

YOU MUST CHOOSE!

SPA MENU

The Deity invites you to enjoy a spa weekend. He hands you an itinerary and firmly reminds you the choices are mandatory.

Would you rather take...

a sewage mudbath

OR

a human sweat Jacuzzi?

Would you rather...

get staple gun acupuncture

OR

get a whale sperm facial?

YOU MUST CHOOSE!

Would you rather...

receive an erotic massage

OR

receive a neurotic massage?

Beauty & Fashion

YOU MUST CHOOSE!

Would you rather...

always display a prominently visible Hanes granny panty line

OR

always wear a shirt slightly too short and pants a waist-size too small so you display a "muffin top" all the time?

Would you rather...

own a pair of sunglasses that give you the ability to spot items on sale from a distance (the way thermal imaging goggles work)

OR

never again run out of clean underwear?

YOU MUST CHOOSE!

Would you rather...

wear an eye patch for a year

OR

wear a nicotine patch for the rest of your life?

Things to consider: what about a nicotine eye patch?

Beauty & Fashion

YOU MUST CHOOSE!

Would you rather...

have eyes that can change color to best match your outfit

OR

have fingernails that can change length and color appropriate for any occasion?

YOU MUST CHOOSE!

Would you rather inherit...

Sarah Palin's campaign suits

OR

the dresses worn by January Jones on Mad Men?

Beauty & Fashion

YOU MUST CHOOSE!

Would you rather...

find out your coveted collection of Jimmy Choo handbags were all cheap knock-offs

OR

your real designer bags were made by slave-like child labor?

YOU MUST CHOOSE!

Would you rather...
have self-renewing shoes
OR
have self-applying make-up?

Would you rather...
have to wear a live spider brooch
OR
tampon earrings?

Beauty & Fashion

YOU MUST CHOOSE!

Would you rather...

have to always go shopping and try on clothes with your mother

OR

have to go shopping and try on clothes with an invective-spitting Stacy and Clinton from *What Not To Wear?*

Would you rather...

own a pair of heels that adjusted to flats with the push of a button

OR

a handbag that was able to carry up to 100 pounds without feeling any heavier?

Beauty & Fashion

YOU MUST CHOOSE!

Would you rather be banned for life from...

Nordstrom **OR** Target?

all department stores **OR** all grocery stores?

Zappos.com **OR** Sephora?

YOU MUST CHOOSE!

Would you rather get an all-you-can-fit-in-your-cart shopping spree at...

Louis Vuitton **OR** Prada?

Banana Republic **OR** Ann Taylor?

Fredericks of Hollywood **OR** Lane Bryant?

Chico's **OR** Forever 21?

Hot Topic **OR** The Salvation Army?

YOU MUST CHOOSE!

Beauty & Fashion

Would you rather...

wear camouflage pattern foundation for a week

OR

mascara the words "Thug" and "Life" on your eye lids?

Would you rather...

always wear a top that left two holes for your nipples

OR

a pair of spandex pants with an ambiguous bulge at the crotch?

YOU MUST CHOOSE!

Would you rather your personal shopper be...

George Clinton **OR** Gilbert Gottfried?

Prince **OR** Bea Arthur?

Cyndi Lauper **OR** Nancy Pelosi?

Beauty & Fashion

YOU MUST CHOOSE!

Would you rather your wardrobe be confined to...

grossly undersized Juicy Couture clothing

OR

JCPenney's maternity wear?

YOU MUST CHOOSE!

Would you rather have...

a goatee transplant

OR

earlobes that connected under your chin?

Beauty & Fashion

YOU MUST CHOOSE!

Would you rather always have to wear...

suspenders adorned with no less than 15 pieces of flair **OR** a tiara?

a marching band's drum attached to your shoulders **OR** orthodontic headgear?

a solid gold grill over your teeth **OR** 14 tubes of lipstick (you can use it wherever as long as it is exposed)?

YOU MUST CHOOSE!

Would you rather...

have the U.S. government mandate the practice of foot binding

OR

require all women to wear burqas?

Beauty & Fashion

YOU MUST CHOOSE!

Would you rather...

have to heavily bedazzle every article of clothing you own

OR

whenever outside, have to wear sunglasses in which each lens is as large as your head?

YOU MUST CHOOSE!

Would you rather...

have the neck of a 90-year old

OR

have the feet of a 90-year old?

Beauty & Fashion

YOU MUST CHOOSE!

Would you rather...

have to wear your shoes on the wrong feet

OR

always have to wear your bra on the outside of your shirt?

Would you rather..

get paid to wear designer outfits like celebrities do

OR

get to be on the red carpet at the Oscars, discussing celebrity wardrobes with Tim Gunn?

YOU MUST CHOOSE!

Would you rather...

wear poorly applied pornstar-length false eyelashes every day to work

OR

wear Borat's neon green stretchy one-piece bathing suit every time you go to the beach?

YOU MUST CHOOSE!

CHAPTER 3

Celebrities & Pop Culture

The Deity is disgusted with our culture's obsession with celebrity; all the hours of potential productivity sacrificed to the worship of talentless, shallow souls who are "famous for being famous." Celebrity gossip is women's porn: a gender-wide time-consuming addiction that leaves one with nothing but a tad of shame. So why not put that addiction to use and choose between two famous-folk fates?

Would you rather elect as president...

Sarah Palin

OR

Tina Fey?

Would you rather...

have the top half of Adriana Lima's body but Aretha Franklin's bottom half

OR

have Salma Hayek's top half but Heather Mills's lower half?

Things to consider: finding dresses that fit, phantom limb syndrome

YOU MUST CHOOSE!

Would you rather your best friend be...

Paris Hilton **OR** Heidi Montag?

Tori Spelling **OR** Tanisha from *The Bad Girls Club*?

Ellen **OR** Tyra?

Anderson Cooper **OR** Tim Gunn?

Celebrities & Pop Culture

YOU MUST CHOOSE!

Would you rather...

when sensing danger, have your lips puff up to the size of Angelina Jolie's

OR

have your butt swell to the size of Jennifer Lopez's?

Things to consider: would you purposely put yourself in danger?

Would you rather...

sew Ellen Page's mouth shut

OR

take away Diablo Cody's computer for life?

YOU MUST CHOOSE!

Would you rather your mom be...

Marge Simpson **OR** Lois Griffin?

Peg Bundy **OR** Morticia Addams?

Nancy Grace **OR** Ann Coulter?

Celebrities & Pop Culture

YOU MUST CHOOSE!

Would you rather your dad be...

Bill Clinton **OR** Richard Gere?

Ru Paul **OR** Ron Paul?

Hulk Hogan **OR** Gandalf?

YOU MUST CHOOSE!

Would you rather suffer the fate of...

Joan of Arc

OR

Katie Holmes?

Would you rather...

have every night out include a visit by the cast of The Hills

OR

every hangover include a visit by the cast of High School Musical?

YOU MUST CHOOSE!

Would you rather...

be caricatured by Kristen Wiig on *Saturday Night Live*

OR

have *Us Weekly* regularly photograph you and make fun of your wardrobe in its *Fashion Police* section?

YOU MUST CHOOSE!

Would you rather...
make out with Tila Tequila
OR
punch her?

Would you rather...
have the heart rate of John McCain
OR
the blink rate of John McCain?

Celebrities & Pop Culture

YOU MUST CHOOSE!

Would you rather your boyfriend be...

Pat O'Brien **OR** Steve-O?

Tom Brady and get chlamydia **OR** Frank Caliendo in the impersonation of your choice?

Michael Phelps **OR** Criss Angel?

Would you rather...

have Jessica Simpson's intellect

OR

Jessica Alba's insatiable need (and respective inability) to be funny?

Things to consider: how difficult Alba makes it for men to masturbate to her in her comedies

YOU MUST CHOOSE!

Would you rather be trapped as a character inside...

Gossip Girl **OR** *Grey's Anatomy?*

Lost **OR** *The View?*

Ugly Betty **OR** *The Office?*

YOU MUST CHOOSE!

Celebrities & Pop Culture

Would you rather...

have Amy Winehouse's drug problems

OR

her fashion problems?

Would you rather...

be added to the cast of *Sex in the City* (during its prime)

OR

Desperate Housewives?

YOU MUST CHOOSE!

Would you rather...

have Angelina Jolie's tattoos

OR

have her kids?

Celebrities & Pop Culture

YOU MUST CHOOSE!

Would you rather swap lives with...

Jenna Bush **OR** Jenna Jameson?

Eva Longoria **OR** Victoria Beckham?

Brigitte Nielsen **OR** Mo'Nique?

YOU MUST CHOOSE!

Would you rather...

be the fourth Kardashian sister

OR

the third Hilton sister?

Would you rather...

have to sit through a drunken tirade from Mel Gibson

OR

a serious religious sermon from Tom Cruise?

Celebrities & Pop Culture

YOU MUST CHOOSE!

Would you rather...

only be able to leave voicemails in the style and manner of an angry Alec Baldwin

OR

only be able to get your hair cut in the style of an angst-ridden Britney Spears?

YOU MUST CHOOSE!

Would you rather...
sit on a transatlantic flight next to Jesus
OR
Oprah?

Things to consider: conversation, mutual armrest competition

Celebrities & Pop Culture

YOU MUST CHOOSE!

Would you rather prevent from ever existing...

guys who imitate Borat **OR** Mike Myers's foreign accented characters?

hip hop moguls **OR** heroin chic supermodels?

Nicole Richie **OR** Rob Schneider?

YOU MUST CHOOSE!

Would you rather attempt to solve...

the atrocities in Darfur with Jennifer Love Hewitt

OR

Planck's Constant with Matt Leblanc?

Celebrities & Pop Culture

YOU MUST CHOOSE!

Would you rather...

have to marry someone at least 40 years older like Woody Allen and Sun-Yi

OR

20 years younger like Demi Moore and Ashton Kutcher?

Things to consider: immaturity, gray pubes

YOU MUST CHOOSE!

Would you rather...

be a Siamese twin with Rachel McAdams **OR** Courtney Cox?

Hillary Duff **OR** Debra Messing?

Condoleezza Rice **OR** Mayor McCheese?

Things to Consider: intelligent conversation, oversized head pushing against you

Would you rather...

hook up with everyone Paris Hilton has ever hooked up

OR

with everyone that Jennifer Aniston has hooked up with?

Would you rather...

date a guy with Mario Lopez's abs and Patrick Dempsey's hair

OR

Jon Stewart's sense of humor and Tommy Lee's penis?

YOU MUST CHOOSE!

Would you rather...

be the personal assistant to Donald Trump
OR
Naomi Campbell?

Things to consider: getting fired, getting tired

Celebrities & Pop Culture

YOU MUST CHOOSE!

Would you rather...

go on a double date with Chris Martin and Gwyneth Paltrow

OR

with Sarah Silverman and Jimmy Kimmel?

YOU MUST CHOOSE!

Would you rather...

perform a karaoke duet with Justin Timberlake

OR

see your mother perform a karaoke duet with T-Pain?

Celebrities & Pop Culture

YOU MUST CHOOSE!

CHAPTER 4

Powers & Fantasies

Good news: The Deity just won a huge pot in a polytheistic game of Texas Hold 'em and he's looking to spread the wealth. He's decided to fulfill a wish—provided that your wish is a meager super power or dubious fantasy. It's a backhanded blessing, sure, but just be grateful that Vishnu didn't have anything higher than two pair up his many sleeves.

Would you rather...

be able to shake off leg hair like a wet dog

OR

reposition fat cells like squeezing a tube of toothpaste?

Things to consider: going outside to shake, molding boobs or butt depending on your date, Popeye forearms for Halloween

Would you rather...

poop fragrant potpourri bundles

OR

have permanent Listerine breath?

YOU MUST CHOOSE!

Would you rather...

be able to automatically dictate your mood just by selecting a MySpace emoticon

OR

instantly be doing whatever you change your Facebook status to?

Powers & Fantasies

YOU MUST CHOOSE!

Would you rather...

have Cameron Diaz's legs **OR** Penelope Cruz's accent?

Tyra Banks's forehead **OR** Tyra Banks's brain?

Kim Kardashian's ass but uncontrollably fart all the time **OR** Salma Hayek's breasts but uncontrollably lactate all the time?

YOU MUST CHOOSE!

Would you rather...

receive a new piece of Tiffany's jewelry every month

OR

receive oral sex from Colin Farrell on your command?

Would you rather have...

the ability to swap facial features with friends

OR

the freedom to swap sexual partners with no emotional or moral fall-out?

YOU MUST CHOOSE!

Would you rather have...

a daily allowance of 10,000 calories with no weight gain

OR

the ability to induce instant and intense diarrhea in anyone you wish?

Things to consider: public debates, dinner parties

Would you rather have...

relationship precognition (know everything that's about to happen)

OR

relationship postcognition (know everything your partner has done)?

Powers & Fantasies

YOU MUST CHOOSE!

Would you rather live in a world...

where women earned on average 25% more money than men

OR

where men experienced menstrual cycles, symptoms and cramps?

Would you rather...

be able to personally choose every member of the Supreme Court

OR

every Oscar winner?

Things to consider: Chief Justice Björk

YOU MUST CHOOSE!

Would you rather be able to have an hour-long chat with...

your 12-year-old self

OR

your 72-year-old self?

Powers & Fantasies

YOU MUST CHOOSE!

Would you rather live in a world...

where men took their wives' last names upon marriage

OR

where couples chose a new last name together?

Things to consider: Maury Chung, Matthew Jessica Parker, Mr. and Mrs. Lightning

YOU MUST CHOOSE!

Would you rather...

have a thumb that dispensed moisturizer

OR

have nipples that can act as cigarette lighters?

Would you rather...

be able to apply make-up through sheer concentration

OR

be able to take away other people's make-up by sheer concentration?

Powers & Fantasies

YOU MUST CHOOSE!

Would you rather have a 3-way with...

Ben and Casey Affleck **OR** Mark and Donnie Wahlberg?

Fred and Ben Savage **OR** Jerry and Charlie O'Connell?

Alf and Smokey the Bear **OR** the Aflac Duck and the Kool-Aid Man?

YOU MUST CHOOSE!

Would you rather...

be able to perform electrolysis with your finger tips

OR

be able to type your thoughts by resting your head on your computer keyboard?

Powers & Fantasies

YOU MUST CHOOSE!

Would you rather...

permanently ban the word "ho" **OR** "dyke"?

"panties" **OR** "bromance"?

the C-word **OR** the N-word?

"windy" **OR** "challenge"?

YOU MUST CHOOSE!

If it meant having a flawless body, would you give up...

eating utensils?

vowels?

carbon-based sexual partners?

Powers & Fantasies

YOU MUST CHOOSE!

Would you rather...

if forced to do so on national TV, with your current abilities, have the chance to nationally disprove the "women are bad drivers" stereotype

OR

the "bad at math" stereotype?

YOU MUST CHOOSE!

Would you rather...

be able to manicure nails by sucking on fingers

OR

pedicure nails by sucking on toes?

Things to consider: doing your own nails, working at a salon

Powers & Fantasies

YOU MUST CHOOSE!

Would you rather...

have access to the world's only honest mechanic

OR

the world's hottest gynecologist?

YOU MUST CHOOSE!

Would you rather...

have an index finger that blended perfect margaritas and other mixed drinks

OR

have card-shuffling cleavage?

Powers & Fantasies

Would you rather...

magically always photograph at your best angle

OR

infallibly execute perfect snap judgment when it comes to selecting an appetizer?

Things to consider: wedding pictures, order envy

YOU MUST CHOOSE!

Bed, Bath, and Beyond

Would you rather...

have a bed that heats on one side but not the other (to mitigate male-female disparity)

OR

have a "toilet blender" (a garbage disposal for your toilet to prevent clogs)?

Would you rather...

have your significant other love to sleep holding, cuddling, and touching you

OR

never have blanket tugging issues?

Powers & Fantasies

YOU MUST CHOOSE!

Would you rather...

receive an all-expense paid trip to Paris but have your travel partner be a two-year-old child you have to look after

OR

spend a romantic luxury private-island escape in Fiji with the two Corey's?

YOU MUST CHOOSE!

Would you rather win...

Class Clown **OR** Best Looking?

Most Likely to Succeed **OR** Most Popular?

Most Weeble-like **OR** Clearly Peaked in High School?

Powers & Fantasies

YOU MUST CHOOSE!

Would you rather...

be able to cause couples to break-up by focusing your negative energy on them

OR

be capable of causing couples to form?

YOU MUST CHOOSE!

Would you rather...
always appear half your age
OR
2/3 of your weight?

Would you rather...
be able to retract your head like a turtle
OR
be able to retract your boobs?

Powers & Fantasies

YOU MUST CHOOSE!

Would you rather...

be able to magically select your hair color and style daily by picking from a book of samples similar to how you would choose carpets

OR

be able to do the same thing with your pubic hair?

YOU MUST CHOOSE!

Would you rather...

have towelettes that can wipe away wrinkles

OR

ones that can wipe away memories of bad relationships?

Powers & Fantasies

YOU MUST CHOOSE!

CHAPTER 5

Weird, Gross, Embarrassing & Painful

The Deity is not pleased. Spurned by the cute barista at the Borders bookstore cafe in Ft. Lee, NJ, he is compelled to vent his anger onto a less powerful mortal and he selects you as the target for his misguided rage. He commands that you suffer a ghastly punishment: an inhuman torture, a bizarre behavioral disorder, an outrageous physical deformity, or just something really, really icky. But to prove he's not a complete male pig, he allows you a choice between two possible fates.

Would you rather have Dick Cheney's...

literal heart

OR

figurative heart?

YOU MUST CHOOSE!

Would you rather...

have all conversation with your boyfriend or husband in the tone of local newscast banter

OR

in the tone of a morning zoo show?

Things to consider: sound effects, wacky guests, "That's great Sheila (chuckle). Now turning our attention to the children..."

YOU MUST CHOOSE!

Weird, Gross, Embarrassing & Painful

Would you rather...

be blow-dried to death

OR

slow-baked to death on a tanning bed?

Things to consider: corpse appearance for funeral

Would you rather...

have a 32°F vagina

OR

150°F nipples?

Things to consider: frozen Vagisil, flammable bras

YOU MUST CHOOSE!

Would you rather...

the National Debt Clock in Times Square instead display your weight at all times

OR

the JumboTron at Madison Square Garden play a video of your daily grooming and waxing regimen?

YOU MUST CHOOSE!

Would you rather...

be limited to having sex with John Goodman until you achieve an orgasm (at which point everyone is fair game)

OR

only be allowed to eat dice until you pooped a 7 (at which point you can eat whatever you want)?

Would you rather...

tongue bathe every Skeeball from a Chuck E. Cheese

OR

handwash the laundry at the *Rock of Love* mansion?

YOU MUST CHOOSE!

Would you rather...

suffer from ingrown eyelashes

OR

eyeball warts?

YOU MUST CHOOSE!

Weird, Gross, Embarrassing & Painful

Would you rather...

upon making any mistake, have someone appear who always sarcastically slow-claps to rub it in

OR

be unable to drink a beverage without doing a spit-take on the first sip?

Things to consider: state dinners, wedding toasts, first dates

YOU MUST CHOOSE!

Would you rather...

emit the sound of nails on a blackboard whenever you scratch an itch

OR

emit the sound of a crying baby whenever you blow your nose?

YOU MUST CHOOSE!

Weird, Gross, Embarrassing & Painful

Would you rather...

have "man hands"

OR

"man feet"?

Would you rather...

slide under your covers, only to discover a dozen roaches scurrying about

OR

sit on the toilet, only to discover a rat swimming around?

YOU MUST CHOOSE!

Would you rather...
use a power drill as a Q-Tip
OR
get a lower back tattoo with lemon juice?

Would you rather...
get a Super Glue facial
OR
use Super Glue as a sexual lubricant?

YOU MUST CHOOSE!

Weird, Gross, Embarrassing & Painful

Would you rather fart ...

in front of your husband/boyfriend **OR** in front of your parents?

in front of your infant child **OR** your pet?

in front of Dame Judi Dench **OR** the ghost of Thomas Jefferson?

YOU MUST CHOOSE!

Would you rather...

have a navel with a Magic 8-Ball readout in it

OR

have barbecue sauce saliva?

Things to consider: combining belly-dancing with fortune-telling, ribs

YOU MUST CHOOSE!

Would you rather get in a catfight with...

Miley Cyrus **OR** Mila Kunis?

NeNe from *Real Housewives Atlanta* **OR** Lauren Conrad from *The Hills*?

Daphne from *Scooby Doo* **OR** Strawberry Shortcake?

YOU MUST CHOOSE!

Would you rather...

bite into a popsicle with your front teeth

OR

snort a spoonful of cayenne pepper?

Would you rather have your breasts have the consistency of...

softballs **OR** partially-wadded tin foil?

bags of Frosted Flakes **OR** a sac of wine?

soap bubbles **OR** solid brass?

YOU MUST CHOOSE!

Weird, Gross, Embarrassing & Painful

Would you rather...

always look like you're severely constipated

OR

always look as if you're miming trying to keep a basketball spinning on your finger?

YOU MUST CHOOSE!

Would you rather...

grow an extra one-inch layer of flesh for every year of your life like a tree grows wood

OR

shed your skin and hair every autumn?

Would you rather...

consume a mouse smoothie

OR

a tarantula wrap?

YOU MUST CHOOSE!

Would you rather have...

your nipples dipped in liquid nitrogen and shattered

OR

your earlobes clipped off with garden hedgers?

Would you rather...

eat Squirrel Intestine Alfredo

OR

a Bull Testicle Parmigiana sandwich?

YOU MUST CHOOSE!

Would you rather...

have to do the Stairmaster for four hours every day for six months

OR

let 40 pounds of a Nautilus weights come crashing down on your fingers just once?

YOU MUST CHOOSE!

Would you rather...

have Meg Ryan's cosmetic surgeon

OR

Madonna's spiritual advisor?

Would you rather...

have three-inch long, finely manicured fingernails

OR

nails of typical length, but yellow and fungified?

YOU MUST CHOOSE!

Would you rather wear...

a bra of maggots

OR

a thong of live eels?

Would you rather...

carry your baby to term on the top of your head

OR

in your butt?

Things to consider: top hats, sitting

Would you rather...

spend an entire day taking backlogged Cosmo quizzes

OR

write a 20-page dissertation on Jon Cryer's character in *Two and a Half Men*?

YOU MUST CHOOSE!

Would you rather...

always use a lidless public toilet

OR

a curtainless shower?

Would you rather...

dive on a Slip-N-Slide covered in sheep excrement and urine

OR

get a Mentos and Diet Coke enema?

YOU MUST CHOOSE!

Would you rather...

speak like a wise Native American chief whenever you're chilly

OR

sprout facial hair at the first sign of traffic, with it getting worse as road congestion increases?

YOU MUST CHOOSE!

Would you rather...

have the arm waddle of the world's fattest woman

OR

have the varicose leg veins of the world's oldest woman?

Things to consider: possible flight?

Would you rather...

be smacked in the face with an Andy Roddick serve and then make out with him

OR

get kicked in the stomach by David Beckham and then grope each other feverishly?

YOU MUST CHOOSE!

Would you rather...

invariably get stuck behind someone at least 11-inches taller than you at every movie, concert, play, etc.

OR

invariably get stuck behind Slowface Johnson whenever you need to get somewhere fast on the street, at an airport, etc.?

YOU MUST CHOOSE!

Would you rather...

have a perpetual watch glint shining in your eyes

OR

be compelled to whistle "Camptown Races" whenever seeing something purple?

YOU MUST CHOOSE!

Would you rather...

have literal crow's feet around your eyes

OR

have horizontal stripes tattooed from your waist to your thighs?

Would you rather...

have your home furnished by the set decorator on *Sanford and Son*

OR

have a nude Chuck Woolery photoshopped into all of your wedding photos?

YOU MUST CHOOSE!

Would you rather...
grow a pimple for every impure thought
OR
sprout a gray hair for every wise one?

Would you rather...
take your measurements 34-28-35 (for example) and have them randomly mixed up
OR
gain five pounds in one random place on your body?

YOU MUST CHOOSE!

Would you rather...

have a type of Tourette's syndrome that causes you to exclaim "Yeah, Boyeeee!" every twenty minutes at work or school

OR

that causes you to exclaim "Here, diagonally!" every minute during sex?

YOU MUST CHOOSE!

Would you rather...

have to make your Number 2's in the shower

OR

have to use cat vomit as conditioner?

Would you rather...

be stranded in shark infested waters with a 10% chance of attack

OR

be stuck in a room with a rabid Janice Dickinson with a 90% chance of attack?

YOU MUST CHOOSE!

Weird, Gross, Embarrassing & Painful

Would you rather...

buy seven cucumbers and three boxes of Vagisil at the supermarket counter

OR

be a nude model for a kindergarten art class?

Would you rather...

bitch slap a polar bear

OR

spit in the eye of an alligator?

YOU MUST CHOOSE!

Would you rather...

have kankles (no distinction between your calves and ankles)

OR

a nin (no distinction between your neck and chin)?

YOU MUST CHOOSE!

Would you rather...

have an upside down vagina **OR** a double-sized vagina?

a half-size vagina **OR** an anus and vagina that have switched places

a vagina that can act as a blowdryer **OR** a vacuum?

YOU MUST CHOOSE!

Would you rather permanently speak...

'70s jive

OR

CSI: Miamese (a language based on David Caruso's wry comments and bad puns)?

Things to consider: "Up top, Blood!"; "It's about time this garbage man... gets recycled."

YOU MUST CHOOSE!

Shop 'Til You...

The Deity, spiritual being that he is, is not a fan of rampant consumerism. So he's adding a detail to your shopping spree to make you reconsider your materialistic ways.

While shopping in department stores, would you rather always...

have to carry a 50-pound handbag

OR

have to wear eight-inch stiletto heels?

YOU MUST CHOOSE!

Would you rather...

do your bathing suit shopping with Jessica Alba

OR

your housewares shopping with Ron Popeil?

Would you rather...

have an unlimited Starbucks card

OR

have the authority to fire any salesperson at any store any time?

YOU MUST CHOOSE!

Weird, Gross, Embarrassing & Painful

Would you rather...

outfit your entire apartment literally with crates and barrels

OR

pottery and barns?

Would you rather...

buy all your shoes from a children's shoe store

OR

all your pants from a Big&Tall store?

YOU MUST CHOOSE!

Would you rather...

never be able to buy an article of clothing that costs more than $8

OR

less than $200?

YOU MUST CHOOSE!

CHAPTER 6

Workin' 9 to 5(ish)

The Deity has empathy for the working class. After all, he's more than willing to remind you of that time he took the form of a floor manager at a Blockbuster Video. He still has the khakis. The Deity shudders to think of what it's like working 40 hours a week without opening your femoral artery. It's for that reason he has decided to give you a chance to spice things up.

Would you rather...

be the CEO of a Fortune 500 company

OR

be the wife of one?

Things to consider: Be honest

Would you rather...

shatter the glass ceiling

OR

watch your boss literally plummet ten stories through one?

YOU MUST CHOOSE!

Would you rather...

work off of a computer from 1978

OR

have to dress in the fashion of 1978?

Things to consider: green text, green bellbottoms

Workin' 9 to 5(ish)

YOU MUST CHOOSE!

Would you rather...

during each night, have your computer's keyboard keys randomized

OR

have little elves always hide your car keys somewhere in your house which you have to find each morning?

Would you rather...

have an office kitty

OR

an office hottie?

Things to consider: tongue baths, visible scratches

Would you rather have co-workers that constantly quoted...

The Simpsons **OR** *Monty Python?*

Grandmaster Flash **OR** *Dianetics?*

Sean Hannity **OR** a calculus textbook?

Workin' 9 to 5(ish)

YOU MUST CHOOSE!

Would you rather...

your office pipe in smooth jazz
OR
the pungent smell of apple pie?

YOU MUST CHOOSE!

Would you rather...

be able to type 80 words per minute with two fingers

OR

be able to type 300 words per minute with your breasts?

Things to consider: level of cubicle privacy, carpal tunnel of the tit

Workin' 9 to 5(ish)

YOU MUST CHOOSE!

Assuming a 5-day work week, would you rather make...

$30,000 as a teacher **OR** $60,000 as a grave digger?

$20,000 as a British food critic **OR** $80,000 as a fecal sculptor?

$40,000 as an obscene shadow puppeteer **OR** $100,000 as a baby seal taxidermist?

YOU MUST CHOOSE!

Would you rather...

work under 1985 office dress codes

OR

1955 office politics?

Things to consider: feathered hair, expectant ass-slapping, "Thanks, babe!"

Would you rather have your office ban...

social networking **OR** instant messages?

handbags **OR** makeup?

bras **OR** sweets?

YOU MUST CHOOSE!

Workin' 9 to 5(ish)

Without anyone finding out, would you sleep with your boss for...

a promotion?

a fully paid, 4-day work week?

a fully paid, 3-day work week?

a gorgeous private work bathroom?

a job title of "Royal Highness"?

YOU MUST CHOOSE!

Would you rather...

increase your annual salary by $1,000

OR

permanently reduce someone else's (your choice) by $10,000?

YOU MUST CHOOSE!

Would you rather...

realize after your first day at work that you were showing serious thong "whale tale"

OR

give a thoughtful presentation only to then realize you had a serious case of nipple-itis during the whole thing?

Things to consider: Both happened to Madeline Albright

YOU MUST CHOOSE!

Would you rather...

people at work think of you as a model employee

OR

people at work think you should be employed as a model?

Workin' 9 to 5(ish)

YOU MUST CHOOSE!

Would you rather...

find out all your emails were being monitored and read by your boss

OR

that all your moments at your desk were being filmed by a security camera?

Would you rather...

have your desk phone ringer set to a *Scooby Doo* yelp

OR

a heavy metal guitar lick?

YOU MUST CHOOSE!

Would you rather...

have to get around the office by crab-walking

OR

have to always coordinate to go the bathroom on a dual toilet with your boss?

Workin' 9 to 5(ish)

YOU MUST CHOOSE!

Would you rather...

be able to go to work in your pajamas

OR

be permitted to tell any co-worker off without consequences?

Would you rather...

have secret access to everyone's IM's

OR

everyone's BM's?

YOU MUST CHOOSE!

Would you rather your workplace implement...

nap time

OR

show and tell?

Things to consider: spooning, productive afternoons, your new nifty hole-puncher

Workin' 9 to 5(ish)

YOU MUST CHOOSE!

CHAPTER 7

More SEX

Fueled by a case of Coors Light and a four-hour block of women's beach volleyball on ESPN2, the Deity's mind has once again gravitated toward carnal matters. It's time for another orgiastic romp of questions. Enjoy the sloppy seconds.

Would you rather...

be able to projectile-lactate with the power of a Super Soaker squirt gun

OR

have nipples of all sorts of sizes and shapes that can be detached and attached like drill bits?

Things to consider: fighting crime, being in a "silver dollar" mood

YOU MUST CHOOSE!

Would you rather have sex with...

Patrick Dempsey **OR** Jon Hamm?

Masi Oka **OR** Rainn Wilson?

George Clooney **OR** Zac Efron?

More SEX

YOU MUST CHOOSE!

Would you rather have sex with...

a hyper-critical Chef Gordon Ramsay **OR** R. Kelly after drinking three Super Big Gulps?

Spencer from *The Hills* **OR** David Beckham wearing a fairly realistic mask of your father's face?

Drew Carey **OR** Ed Westwick after soaking in pickle brine for 24 hours?

YOU MUST CHOOSE!

Would you rather have a threesome with...

any two Jonas brothers **OR** any two Baldwin brothers?

Ashlee Simpson and Luke Wilson **OR** Jessica Simpson and Owen Wilson?

Penn and Teller **OR** Hannity and Colmes?

Sharon and Ozzy Osbourne **OR** Wallace and Gromit?

YOU MUST CHOOSE!

Would you rather...

generate squeaky bed noises while having sex no matter where you are having sex

OR

have a romantic ocean tide softly lap into your entwined bodies no matter where you are having sex?

Things to consider: waking the neighbors, constantly drying the sheets

YOU MUST CHOOSE!

Would you rather only be able to masturbate using...

a set of keys **OR** a fudgesicle?

a TV remote control **OR** a set of chopsticks?

cacti **OR** an Alan Alda bobblehead?

More SEX

YOU MUST CHOOSE!

Would you rather date someone with...

an always half-soft 8-inch penis **OR** a rock hard 3-inch penis?

a 1/4-inch wide penis **OR** a 3-inch wide penis

a penis the exact size and shape of a Coke can **OR** the same size and shape of a candy cane?

YOU MUST CHOOSE!

Would you rather...

sit through 60 total hours of your boyfriend's college buddy stories

OR

sit through 10 minutes of his experimentation in golden showers?

More SEX

YOU MUST CHOOSE!

Would you rather...

have a sexual partner who always confused which set of cheeks to spank

OR

have grandparents who always confused which set of cheeks to pinch?

Would you rather...

have a butt you could literally set a drink on

OR

nipples that could actually cut glass when it's cold?

Things to consider: Happy Hour at crowded bars, car theft

YOU MUST CHOOSE!

Would you rather...

have a lesbian encounter with Leighton Meester **OR** Lauren Conrad?

Victoria Beckham **OR** Fergie?

Carrie Underwood **OR** Rachael Ray if she cooked you a four course meal after?

Playboy's *The Girls Next Door* **OR** Ellen DeGeneres and Portia de Rossi?

More SEX

YOU MUST CHOOSE!

If you shined a blacklight in your partner's house, would you rather find splotches...

on pictures of men in *Sports Illustrated* **OR** on pictures of your best friend?

on family reunion pictures **OR** on your favorite cereal bowl?

on his John Adams biography **OR** on various maps and globes but always in Uruguay?

YOU MUST CHOOSE!

Would you rather...

have sex with an in-character Stephen Colbert

OR

an in-character Keifer Sutherland?

YOU MUST CHOOSE!

Would you rather only be able to achieve orgasm with...

Unibomber impersonators **OR** Arby's employees named LaMont?

white hip hop wannabee teens **OR** 400-pound men?

sporks **OR** Yahtzee dice and mugs?

Would you rather...

have self-moisturizing skin

OR

have a self-maintaining vagina?

YOU MUST CHOOSE!

Would you rather...

have only female sex partners

OR

have only male friends?

On your first date, would you rather be taken to...

a Bible party **OR** a Sci-Fi book club party?

an underground dogfighting operation **OR** his cousin's funeral?

his air guitar tournament **OR** Home Depot?

YOU MUST CHOOSE!

Would you rather...

discover that your partner had a secret meth addiction

OR

that he's the bassist in a Creed cover band?

YOU MUST CHOOSE!

Would you rather...

French kiss Clive Owen **OR** give Jude Law a handjob?

receive oral sex from Greg Kinnear **OR** go down on Javier Bardem?

get a Dirty Sanchez from Delroy Lindo **OR** a Cleveland Steamer from Sir Ben Kingsley?

Would you rather try to change...

Bender from *The Breakfast Club*

OR

Patrick Bateman from *American Psycho*?

YOU MUST CHOOSE!

Would you... have sex with Carrot Top to have sex with Hugh Jackman?

Would you... have sex with Bill Gates to have the next Windows operating system named after you?

Would you... make out with your sibling for five minutes to have sex with three celebrities of your choice?

YOU MUST CHOOSE!

Would you have sex with...

Jay-Z if he was wearing that VISOR that Geordi wore on Star Trek?

Sacha Baron Cohen with a mild case of the runs?

Leonardo DiCaprio if he had had sex with twenty other women in succession right before?

Brad Pitt in a bed filed with thumbtacks?

Johnny Depp if he had the body of Ron Jeremy?

YOU MUST CHOOSE!

Would you rather marry...

a hapless open mic musician **OR** a successful government assassin?

an accountant with a lazy eye **OR** a neurosurgeon with a wandering eye?

an eco terrorist **OR** a creationist?

YOU MUST CHOOSE!

Would you rather...

see your ex proposing to his new girlfriend on an eHarmony commercial

OR

be dumped via JumboTron at a pro baseball game?

Things to consider: mass humiliation, being consoled by a giant chicken

YOU MUST CHOOSE!

Would you have marathon sex for a weekend with Robert Pattinson in a private villa in Belize if it meant...

catching HPV?

you could not have sex for the next five years?

being $50k in debt?

YOU MUST CHOOSE!

When searching through you boyfriend/husband's drawers, would you rather find...

Rogaine **OR** bad Battlestar Galactica fan fiction?

a hidden-camera video of the two of you having sex that said 1 of 10,000 copies **OR** a hidden-camera video of him and someone else?

drugs **OR** a bag containing every tissue he ever used?

YOU MUST CHOOSE!

CHAPTER 8

Random Play

Who says it's women who are moody? The Deity has set his questions on shuffle, so just cross your fingers and hope for something non-permanent.

Would you rather...

have a magical pout that can make anyone forgive you

OR

have a magical booty shake that can jumpstart a car?

YOU MUST CHOOSE!

Would you... accept equal rights but never be able to wear another piece of jewelry again?

Would you... have a threesome with your best friend?

Random Play

YOU MUST CHOOSE!

Would you rather...

have your nightly plans Twittered to your parents

OR

have your parents' nightly thoughts Twittered to you?

Would you rather...

have underarm hair that grows at the rate of one-inch per minute

OR

drool 12 ounces of saliva every minute?

Things to consider: terrycloth clothing, always pretending you're drinking water

YOU MUST CHOOSE!

Would you rather...

need your first-grade teacher there praising you to be able you use the bathroom

OR

grab random objects, say what they are, and hand them to people like a two-year-old does?

Would you rather...

have nipples that have grown into each other

OR

suffer unrelenting panic attacks every time you hear the word "cheese"?

YOU MUST CHOOSE!

Would you rather...

clog the toilet the first time you go to your boyfriend/husband's parents house

OR

fart loudly during your first dinner with them?

Would you rather...

have to bathe yourself like a cat

OR

have to relieve yourself in a litter box like a cat?

YOU MUST CHOOSE!

Would you rather...

have Sisqo's "Thong Song" play whenever you enter a room

OR

whenever you're being introduced to someone, be compelled to feverishly lick their face?

Things to consider: pretending you come from a foreign country with different traditions

Random Play

YOU MUST CHOOSE!

Would you rather...

never again lose a pair of sunglasses but always receive a mild electric shock when using a slotted spoon

OR

always get to fly in First Class, but during the flight believe you are Biz Markie?

YOU MUST CHOOSE!

Would you rather...

have Mariah Carey's body but speak in her vocal histrionics

OR

have Elisabeth Hasselbeck's face but think in her shortsighted logic?

Random Play

YOU MUST CHOOSE!

Would you rather your only friends be...

the women from the Glade scented candle commercials

OR

the men from the FreeCreditReport.com commercials?

Would you rather...

gain access to any club but have to wear a Mexican wrestler's mask while inside

OR

always have a designated driver but be regulated to a motorcycle sidecar?

YOU MUST CHOOSE!

Would you rather...

own an apartment in Florence but be compelled to moan very sexually when in agreement with someone

OR

be able to effortlessly mount and dismount hammocks but be incapable of refraining from singing that racist (duh-duh-duh-duh-duh-duh-duh-duh-duh) song at Asians?

YOU MUST CHOOSE!

Would you rather...

possess an innate ability to select the best-valued wine but never be able to master an "inside voice"

OR

have an enviable collection of Girl Scout merit badges but find every FAQ personally condescending?

YOU MUST CHOOSE!

Would you rather your four-year-old child's babysitter be...

Andy Dick

OR

Gary Busey?

Random Play

YOU MUST CHOOSE!

On your wedding day, would you rather...

find the groom doing tongue gymnastics with the maid of honor

OR

find your dad's head in the priest's lap?

YOU MUST CHOOSE!

Would you rather be raised...

by a pack of wolves

OR

a pack of Wolf Blitzers?

Things to consider: the thrill of the antelope chase, the excitement of a senatorial race

Would you rather watch...

Hostel just before your Eurorail vacation

OR

the plane crash scene in *Alive* during your flight?

YOU MUST CHOOSE!

Because everyone has an opinion... there's a *Would You Rather...?* title for everyone!

The media obsessed:

People who can't get enough of a good thing:

The romantically-inclined:

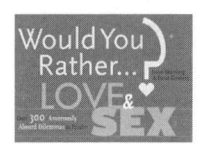

People who REALLY can't get enough of a good thing:

People on the go:

People who prefer pictures to words:

All kids:

People obsessed with money:

All kids, but mostly boys:

www.wouldyourather.com
www.sevenfooter.com